HOW TO
OPERATE
IN THE
GIFTS
OF THE
SPIRIT

HOW TO
OPERATE
IN THE
GIFTS
OF THE
SPIRIT

STEVEN BROOKS

DESTINY IMAGE® PUBLISHERS, INC.

P.O. Box 310, Shippensburg, PA 17257-0310

"Promoting Inspired Lives."

This book and all other Destiny Image, Revival Press, MercyPlace, Fresh Bread, Destiny Image Fiction, and Treasure House books are available at Christian bookstores and distributors worldwide.

For a U.S. bookstore nearest you, call 1-800-722-6774.

For more information on foreign distributors, call 717-532-3040.

Reach us on the Internet: www.destinyimage.com.

ISBN 13 TP: 978-0-7684-4248-9

ISBN 13 Ebook: 978-0-7684-8457-1

For Worldwide Distribution, Printed in the U.S.A.

3 4 5 6 7 8 / 18 17 16 15 14

DEDICATION

This book is dedicated to all the saints who desire to be used by God in the spiritual gifts. May the Holy Spirit flow through you to minister the gifts to strengthen God's people and minister the love of Christ to the lost.

CONTENTS

1

THE MOST IMPORTANT PERSON ON THE EARTH TODAY

As we begin our journey of how to operate in the spiritual gifts we must look to the Lord Jesus who has provided a special person to assist us along the way. I would like to share with you briefly about the most important person on the earth today. This person is not the president of the United States, nor is it a prime minister of another country. It is not the CEO of any major corporation, nor is it anyone on the top 100 list of the wealthiest people in the world. It is not any well-known religious leader or television or movie personality. The most important person on the earth today is the Holy Spirit.

The Heavenly Father is in heaven seated on His glorious throne. At His right hand is seated the Son who is Jesus Christ. When Jesus fulfilled His earthly ministry of providing a way of redemption for lost humankind through His death, burial, and resurrection at Calvary, He then left the planet. But He did not leave us on our own; He sent the Holy Spirit to abide with us forever.

When you read through the whole Bible from the book of Genesis on through to Revelation, you see that in the Old Testament the Heavenly Father is clearly revealed. When you begin in the New Testament, you see in the four Gospels that Jesus is the center of attention. But from the book of Acts and onward, you see the work of the Holy Spirit emphasized.

The Holy Spirit is a person. He is not a fog or a vapor that has no shape or form. He is not a dove or a pigeon. He is not a ghost, nor is He an "it" or a "thing." The Holy Spirit has a will and a mind. He can be grieved when Christians do wrong and He can rejoice when Christians do what is right. He can speak, and His primary ministry is to bear witness of Jesus. The Old Testament Hebrew word *ruwach* was used when talking about the Spirit. This word means "wind." In the New Testament the Greek word *pneuma* was used which means "breath" or a "breeze." Therefore the Holy Spirit can be viewed as being the "Wind of God" or "Breath of God."

In the Western church we think more often of the Holy Spirit as being representative of fire. This would be related to Acts chapter 2 when the Holy Spirit came upon the 120 believers with tongues of fire. Often if you watch American ministers in meetings they will shout "The fire of God is on you!" But in other parts of the world some cultures relate to Him better as the "Wind of God." For example, in South India the temperature can rise well over 110 degrees Fahrenheit and include sweltering humidity. Many people do not have air-conditioning so the blistering heat is very uncomfortable. In these hot conditions they do not desire more heat, but they greatly want to be cooled off. So to the believers there, they view the Holy Spirit as the "Breeze of God" who cools and refreshes them.

The Holy Spirit is a real person just as you and me, but He is God. He is the third Person of the Godhead, which is also known as the Holy Trinity consisting of the Father, Son, and the Holy Spirit.

Three distinct and separate individuals, yet they divinely function as one God. The following verse demonstrates that the Holy Spirit is God.

> *But Peter said, "Ananias, why has Satan filled your heart to lie to the Holy Spirit and keep back part of the price of the land for yourself? While it remained, was it not your own? And after it was sold, was it not in your own control? Why have you conceived this thing in your heart? You have not lied to men but to God"* (Acts 5:3-4).

Peter told Ananias that when he lied to the Holy Spirit he lied to God. The Holy Spirit is God. The Holy Spirit is the person who carries out the will of God and He is boundless in power.

Mary was a virgin who was not yet married. The angel Gabriel appeared to her and told her that she would conceive in her womb and bring forth a son named Jesus who would reign over an eternal kingdom. Shocked by this announcement, Mary asked Gabriel how this could be.

> *And the angel answered and said to her, "The Holy Spirit will come upon you, and the power of the Highest will overshadow you; therefore, also, that Holy One who is to be born will be called the Son of God* (Luke 1:35).

Mary was miraculously impregnated by the Holy Spirit who placed the seed of Jesus within her. This was not done through a sexual act, but by the Holy Spirit overshadowing her. The word "overshadow" can be translated as "a shining cloud." This is the same description we see used by the Jews to describe the manifested presence of God in the Old Testament that was known as the "Shekinah" glory. The Holy Spirit came upon Mary in a brilliant cloud of glory and from that moment on she was pregnant with Jesus. Sometimes

I find it a little bit humorous concerning the weak attempts that the devil makes to emulate God with counterfeit efforts. The Jewish historian Josephus lived shortly after the time of Jesus and he recorded much about the history of the Jews, the Roman emperors, and the fall of Jerusalem in A.D. 70. Josephus shares a true story that is somewhat comical in its nature because it contrasts how different the gods of other religions and their followers are, as opposed to the absolute purity of the Holy Spirit.

According to Josephus there was a woman in Rome whose name was Paulina. She was very rich and of a beautiful countenance. She was married to Saturnius who had a very good reputation in the city. But a man named Mundus greatly desired to have Paulina. He was very successful in business and he offered her 200,000 Attic drachmae (about $100,000 in today's currency) if she would sleep with him for one night. Paulina already had wealth and was married so she refused his request, despite continual gifts being sent to her by Mundus in great abundance.

When Mundus saw that his hope had been lost, he decided to starve himself to death. Mundus had a former slave girl named Ida who still worked for him who was very crafty. She knew that Paulina worshiped at the temple of Isis. Ida went to the temple of Isis and bribed the priest with 25,000 Attic drachmae. She assured the priests that the matter would be concealed and that they would receive more money from Mundus once the plan was carried out. The priests agreed to help deceive Paulina.

A message from the temple priest was sent to inform Paulina that the god Anubis (Isis and Anubis were both Egyptian gods) had requested Paulina to dine and sleep that night at the temple. She went to the temple and had dinner. As it became dark the priests closed the doors and put the lights out. Mundus, who had been hiding, then jumped out under the cover of darkness and revealed himself as being

Anubis. Throughout the night Mundus had his way with Paulina, while the whole time she assumed he was a god.

Two days later Mundus revealed to Paulina what really happened in the temple. When she told her husband he was furious and reported it to the emperor. Tiberius the emperor had both of the priests and Ida crucified and then had the temple of Isis torn down and the statue of Isis thrown into the river. Mundus got off rather lightly and only received exile, because his act was considered a crime of passion.

A primary difference between the God of the Bible and all the other millions of gods that are worshiped in the earth today is that only the God of the Bible is holy. There is no other god that directs its followers to lead holy lives and turn away from sin. This is why God's Spirit is called the *Holy* Spirit. Some world religions do not even mention the concept of sin, but take an opposite position of God and say there is no such thing as sin. However, the Holy Spirit will never lead a person to do anything in opposition to the word of God—the Bible. The Holy Spirit would never lead a married woman to have a sexual encounter with another man. The God I serve would never tell my wife to go to a temple and remove her clothes like Paulina was led to believe. God is holy and He calls His people to live holy lives. By learning to be friends with the Holy Spirit we can discover how to please God in all that we do.

> *The grace of the Lord Jesus Christ, and the love of God,*
> *and the communion of the Holy Spirit be with you all.*
> *Amen* (2 Corinthians 13:14).

The word communion in its full meaning can be understood as "fellowship, sharing in communication, sharing in all aspects of life." As a believer, the Holy Spirit lives within you and He wants to be your friend, comforter, guide, and advisor. This ongoing fellowship can be very sweet and rewarding. It produces the fruit of the Spirit and it also allows the gifts of the Spirit to come forth abundantly.

You may not know everything there is in the Bible. People may not have knowledge of much of the Bible if they are new believers. But the Holy Spirit has written the law of God upon our hearts, and He will let you know on the inside if something is wrong, or something that you should not participate in. He also grants a wonderful peace within your heart when everything is right and is pleasing to God.

God wants you to be filled with the Holy Spirit. Being filled with the Spirit is much more than just speaking in tongues. It is being able to live the life that God has called you to in the fullest measure. The life that comes forth when you are filled with the Spirit is far above the carnal life that even some Christians choose to walk in.

> For to be carnally minded is death, but to be spiritu-ally minded is life and peace. Because the carnal mind is enmity against God; for it is not subject to the law of God, nor indeed can be. So then, those who are in the flesh cannot please God (Romans 8:6-8).

The phrase "carnally minded" refers to thinking with the fleshly mind that is not conformed to the knowledge of God. The word "carnal" means "flesh." It refers to man's natural way of thinking that excludes God out of the thought processes. Our English word carnal has its roots in the Latin word "meat." When Apostle Paul was refer-ring to those with "carnal minds," he was basically saying they were "meat heads." That may sound shocking, but that is how far apart the mind of sinful humanity is compared to the mind of God. Paul said the carnal mind is "enmity" toward God. The word "enmity" is very similar to our English word "enemy." It implies hatred toward God and the way He operates. When you are filled with the Spirit you become a friend of God and you work with Him—not against

Him. We are commanded by God to be filled with the Spirit. This is not a suggestion, but rather a requirement necessary to live a victorious life.

> *And do not be drunk with wine, in which is dissipation; but be filled with the Spirit* (Ephesians 5:18).

I also like how the Weymouth Translation translates this verse.

> *Do not over-indulge in wine—a thing in which excess is so easy—but drink deeply of God's Spirit* (Ephesians 5:18 WNT).

There is a contrast used here to steer people away from drunkenness associated with alcohol to the infilling of the Holy Spirit. I've known people who are very reserved in their normal everyday behavior. But I've also seen some of these people at weddings and watched as their behavior changed dramatically when they consumed alcohol. They went from mild to wild in less than one hour. Later they felt embarrassed for their funny but crude behavior. Often at airports I've noticed total strangers at the restaurant bar act like they are best friends because it's "Happy Hour." They are drinking as many cocktails and as much beer as they can because drinks are half price. The drunker they become the friendlier they get.

Most people want to live in a perpetual "Happy Hour" where the problems of life are pushed away and a person feels free and joyful. It's possible to have this when you are filled with the Holy Spirit. Once I went to minister with my wife in Temecula, California, which has beautiful wineries scattered throughout the county. I wasn't sure what the message was that the Lord wanted me to share that Sunday morning, but as we drove toward the church I kept seeing all of the vineyards and the grapes ripening in the warm sun. It came into my heart that I should preach about the Holy Spirit. The church where I was ministering was comprised of former alcoholics and drug addicts who came to Christ and found salvation.

The pastor at this church was very strong in his walk with the Lord, but it was apparent many of the members were weak in their faith. These people all dearly loved the Lord but they were in need of deliverance to help them overcome many of the strongholds that still persisted in their lives. That morning I taught about the Holy Spirit and shared the importance of being filled with the Spirit. After ministering God's Word to them, I asked if anyone wanted to be filled with the Spirit. To my joy almost the entire church responded. That morning many were baptized in the Holy Spirit, spoke with tongues, were filled with laughter, and quite a number of physical healings took place. What a difference the Holy Spirit makes. Those who previously found joy in alcohol now found something much, much better. They found that the joy of the Lord is their strength. This pastor was open to allowing me to move in the Spirit and to let God do something fresh and new.

I think one of the saddest things in the world is for a pastor to not allow the Holy Spirit to move as He desires in the church. When the Holy Spirit is quenched, a cold and formal religion will set in and the hearts of the people become dull. If you are filled with the Spirit, you will always maintain your edge. Your spiritual axe will always be sharp and you will swing it with wisdom and efficiency. You will find that the devil cannot catch you off guard because your walk with God is vibrant.

The underlying principle of being filled with the Spirit is being full of the joy that God gives, which is then expressed outwardly through songs that glorify the Lord. When you are filled with the joy of the Lord you are a mighty witness for the gospel of Christ. Others will want to come and drink from the source of your joy and find out where you have your "Happy Hour."

And Nehemiah, who was the governor, Ezra the priest and scribe, and the Levites who taught the people said to all the people, "This day is holy to the Lord your God; do not mourn nor weep." For all the people wept, when they heard the words of the Law. Then he said to them, "Go your way, eat the fat, drink the sweet, and send portions to those for whom nothing is prepared; for this day is holy to our Lord. Do not sorrow, for the joy of the Lord is your strength" (Nehemiah 8:9-10).

When the Israelites heard the Law of God as it was read to them by their leaders, they began to weep because they were grieved for their sins. Nevertheless, the religious leaders encouraged the people to maintain their joy because the Lord wanted His people to celebrate the Feasts of Tabernacles, which was at hand. The devil never likes it when God's people are happy. The devil wants you to be miserable and constantly expecting something bad to happen to you. The devil wants you to be depressed since he is in a deep depression because he has been eternally condemned—he knows his final outcome and the judgment that awaits him. If the devil can steal your joy then he can rob you of your spiritual strength, because joy and spiritual strength are intimately connected. I grew up in church and the devil robbed us of our joy through religious tradition. Church was somber and heavy. We were thankful we were saved, but we found ourselves emotionally suppressed and inwardly shut down. Even the songs we sang carried a note of despair.

We often sang one particular song when we were just about to dismiss from church. It was considered a closing song because it was written to be mindful of Jesus while we were outside of the church. The song started out with these self-defeating words:

17

Take the Name of Jesus with you,
Child of sorrow and of woe.

We probably sang that song several hundred times over the years while attending church in my youth. We were taught from the pulpit that to be Christians we were to expect our lives to be full of sorrow, woe, and crushing defeat—then one day we would die and go to heaven where it will, as the preacher gravely said, "finally all be over with."

Once while talking with a minister friend of mine who grew up in the United Kingdom, we discussed some of the songs we learned in church when we were young. We could now clearly see how the words of those songs depleted us of the little joy we clung to the more we sang them. She told me there was a song they sang often in her church that had the following chorus, which was sung with unsmiling and vinegary faces. The chorus was repeated over and over and goes as follows:

Worms, worms, worms,
We're all just worms,
Coming before the throne of grace.

You can easily imagine that if you sang that song continually how low your self-esteem would be. Thank God we are not worms and thank God we do not have to live with a "woe is me" mentality. Because we are in Christ we have been made kings and priests, and we have a reason to hold up our heads and not be ashamed of our eternal inheritance.

The reason the church slips into spiritual dryness is because of not honoring the Holy Spirit. The Holy Spirit is the author of the Bible. He is the breath of God. He brings life to everything He touches. If there is no life, it is because the Holy Spirit is not allowed access to release the joy of the Lord. The fruit of the Spirit is joy. Joy is not the fruit of the devil. The Holy Spirit wants to fill you to overflowing and make you joyful.

In light of the Scriptures, should not Christians be the happiest people on earth? When God makes you happy and you are filled up with the Spirit, then songs will begin to flow out of you. It's almost impossible to shut it down. It's like a well springing up inside you. When this occurs, sing those songs to the Lord and worship Him. It has nothing to do with the sound of your voice or whether or not you are a good singer. God wants your praise. He wants to fill you to overflowing. He desires to bless you because He loves you.

> *Speaking to one another in psalms and hymns and spiritual songs, singing and making melody in your heart to the Lord* (Ephesians 5:19).

Sometimes these spiritual songs come out during the middle of the night. You get up to go to the restroom at 3 o'clock in the morning and a song begins to bubble up out of you. Go ahead and praise the Lord, even if you have to do so quietly so others are not disturbed.

> *I call to remembrance my song in the night; I meditate within my heart, and my spirit makes diligent search* (Psalm 77:6).

No one can stay full of the Holy Spirit all of the time. The trials and difficulties of life cause us to need those times of refilling. When we realize we are running low on oil, then we need to get filled up again. Whenever a few months pass by, I notice that eventually the "oil" light in my vehicle appears indicating that I need to have the oil changed. I guess it's just human nature to delay in getting this needful task accomplished. But the sooner we get this done, the better our engine will operate.

From a spiritual perspective we need to have the clean golden oil of the Spirit inside us. If the oil in a vehicle has not been changed for a long time it becomes a dark and dirty color and full of impurities. Worse than having grimy oil that can no longer work effectively is having no oil at all. King David knew what it meant to get a fresh anointing. The Holy Spirit was often presented in the Old Testament through the symbolism of oil.

> *But my horn You have exalted like a wild ox; I have been anointed with fresh oil* (Psalm 92:10).

David also knew how to relax and let God refresh him as he took a break from battle and enjoyed the Lord's provision.

> *You prepare a table before me in the presence of my enemies; You anoint my head with oil...* (Psalm 23:5).

Even the apostles in the early church knew the importance of being continually filled with the Spirit. We see their initial infilling on the day of Pentecost, recorded in the book of Acts the second chapter, when the Holy Spirit came into the room with such power that it sounded like a mighty rushing wind had blown in. Tongues of fire settled on them and they were all filled with the Holy Spirit. Later we see that they were filled again after a time of prayer. If the apostles and the early church received consecutive infillings, then we should as well.

> *And when they had prayed, the place where they were assembled together was shaken; and they were all filled with the Holy Spirit, and they spoke the word of God with boldness* (Acts 4:31).

We can conclude from this verse that one of the leading ways to receive a fresh infilling is to have a strong prayer life. Without an active prayer life you can never have a close walk with God. The Holy Spirit would like to become your best friend—but the initiative is yours to take by seeking the Lord with all of your heart.

The spiritual gifts originate from the Holy Spirit. We can operate in the gifts while we are full of joy. Actually, you will discover that when you operate in the gifts and then you see others blessed, it will bring a tremendous joy and strength within you.

It is essential that you stay filled with the Spirit so you are on-call and ready to go at any moment that God may choose to work through you. Make it a lifestyle of walking close with God. The closer you get to God, the more the truth will dawn on you that the Holy Spirit really is the most important Person on the earth today. Get ready now for the Holy Spirit to cause His mighty gifts to flow through you!

2

HOW TO OPERATE IN THE GIFTS OF THE HOLY SPIRIT

*Now concerning spiritual gifts, brethren, I do not want
you to be ignorant: You know that you were Gentiles,
carried away to these dumb idols, however you were led.
Therefore I make known to you that no one speaking
by the Spirit of God calls Jesus accursed, and no one
can say that Jesus is Lord except by the Holy Spirit.
There are diversities of gifts, but the same Spirit. There
are differences of ministries, but the same Lord. And
there are diversities of activities, but it is the same
God who works all in all* (1 Corinthians 12:1-6).

The better understanding we have concerning the spiritual gifts,
the stronger manifestations we will have regarding them. This
approach of gaining knowledge about our intended subject would
apply toward any field of study. On the surface we may have a basic

grasp of how something operates, but if we study it diligently then we will have a much better hope of realizing the fullest potential that can be gained of operating in the spiritual gifts.

> *Now concerning spiritual gifts, brethren, I do not want you to be ignorant* (1 Corinthians 12:1).

When Apostle Paul introduced to us the nine spiritual gifts, he expressed his deep desire that we would "not be ignorant" of the gifts. It is possible to be a Christian and sit in church for decades and be absolutely clueless about what the gifts are, how they operate, and how they can be manifested through the believer.

It is not good to be ignorant, misinformed, or unlearned in a subject that can bring such rich blessing into a believer's life. Ignorance is not bliss. Ignorance is missed opportunities and wasted blessings. To be ignorant concerning the spiritual gifts does not mean a person is unintelligent, it simply means they are not properly informed. You must determine to educate yourself concerning spiritual gifts. From a spiritual perspective, God would like you to attain a Ph.D. in the knowledge and operation of the spiritual gifts. The Lord wants you to have a clear and precise understanding of what each gift is, and how it operates. Your diligence to learn this heavenly information will be rewarded to you in ways that cause you to move forward in your calling in life. These gifts will prove vital to helping you accomplish the goals that God has put within your heart. When the gifts are operating in your life, others will desire your friendship and be influenced to seek the Lord because of the spiritual wealth that is found within you.

> *You know that you were Gentiles, carried away to these dumb idols, however you were led. Therefore I make known to you that no one speaking by the Spirit of God calls Jesus accursed, and no one can say that Jesus is Lord except by the Holy Spirit* (1 Corinthian 12:2-3).

Here we see Paul addressing the church in Corinth in reference to their life before they came to know Christ. Many of them formerly were idol worshipers. The city of Corinth was a very hedonistic city. The most famous idol worshiped was Aphrodite, the goddess of love. Aphrodite had her own temple that set high on a hill and employed 1,000 cult prostitutes. The city was loaded with sailors and salesmen who passed through its two major harbors. Near the temple were 33 wine shops. Gross sexual immorality and drunkenness were celebrated in the culture of Corinth.

The second most famous idol worshiped in Corinth was Poseidon. He also had his own temple dedicated to him. Poseidon was considered the god of the sea. He received a lot of worship because the prosperity of Corinth depended upon the sea. Apollo, Hermes, and Isis also had their own temples. There were twelve primary temples, each devoted to the worship of a specific god. Paul called these gods "dumb idols." These idols were speechless. Despite their beautiful temples there was no life in their statues or stone-carved monuments. In this context of understanding the church's former lifestyle of idol worship, Paul said, "no one speaking by the Spirit of God calls Jesus accursed, and no one can say that Jesus is Lord except by the Holy Spirit."

When we study church history we see that there were believers in the church at Corinth who would publicly say things out of place, or say things that were wrong, while thinking they were being influenced by the Holy Spirit. For example, it appears that a believer in the church said, "Jesus is cursed." Well, the Holy Spirit would never influence anyone to say something like that. It is also possible that unbelievers would come in to visit the church, and they would say, "Jesus is Lord." They may have said it, but they didn't understand what they were speaking, so it was not the Holy Spirit who was influencing them to say it. For instance, I have friends who are Hindu. They will tell me that Jesus is the Lord. But while they say this, they also believe that there are millions of other gods who are also Lord. In their understanding Jesus is just another member of the pantheon of gods that exist. So, when they say that "Jesus is Lord," it has no biblical meaning. When people receive Jesus as their Savior and Lord then they can confess with the help of the Holy Spirit that Jesus is Lord.

> *There are diversities of gifts, but the same Spirit* (1 Corinthians 12:4).

The word "diversities" means that each gift has a distinct difference. The nine gifts are each unique in their own special way, but it is the same Holy Spirit who causes them to come forth. The believer and unbeliever both have natural talents that can be discovered and developed. An unbeliever may have a talent to sing or be exceptionally good at math or juggling balls. But only the Christian believer has spiritual gifts. The word "gift" is the Greek word *charismata*. The *charis* part of charismata means "grace." The *ma* part of charismata implies "it is a grace given."

> *There are differences of ministries, but the same Lord* (1 Corinthians 12:5).

Here we are told that there are different kinds of ministries. The word "ministries" is the Greek word *diakonia*. This word means "to serve." It's where we get our English word "deacon." It means to serve and execute the demand of others. We all have different ways of serving. For some people their service of the gifts is carried out on the mission fields of foreign countries. For others it is the college campus or at sporting events. My serving of the gifts takes place primarily to the church body through the different ministry outreaches that the Lord has assigned to me. Some believers serve children, others minister to adults. Paul served the Gentiles, Peter served the Jews. It is possible to have the same gift but a different ministry.

And there are diversities of activities, but it is the same God who works all in all (1 Corinthians 12:6).

There are different kinds of activities. The word "activities" comes from the Greek word *energema*. It is where we get our English word "energy." It refers to the activity, the working, and the operation of a spiritual gift. It expresses how a gift is energized. The operation of a gift can be presented differently from person to person. The human factor comes into play here because we all have different personalities and characteristics. Some people are loud, others are quiet.

Some time back I was ministering in a conference and one of the speakers had a tremendously powerful voice. His voice wasn't just loud, it would better be described as "booming." I could actually sit in my hotel room located on a different floor and also positioned far away from the conference hall and still hear him from my room when it was his time to speak. But that's the way God made him, and it blends well with his style of ministry. Some people have a flair for the dramatic, while others are calm or lean toward a mild personality.

Despite how the gift works, it is the same God who works through each of His people. God did not choose to stamp us all out of a giant cookie cutter mold. You should be thankful for the voice God gave you. You should be happy with the looks God gave you. You should accept and appreciate the height at which you stand— whether short or tall. You are unique for a reason. Be content to be just who you are and there will always be a genuine quality that allows the gift being expressed through you to have more effectiveness toward others.

We see the involvement of the Father, Son, and Holy Spirit in the spiritual gifts. The Holy Spirit manifests the nine different gifts through the believer. The Lord Jesus assigns us with different callings in our service to Him, so that the gifts are taken into all walks of society. The Heavenly Father works out within you the operation of the gifts and oversees all things.

> *But the manifestation of the Spirit is given to each one for the profit of all* (1 Corinthians 12:7).

The *manifestation* of the Spirit is a wonderful thing. I have always enjoyed good preaching and I highly value good teaching. As much as we need good preaching and teaching, we would still feel something missing on the inside if that's *all* we had. Along with the ministry of God's Word we also need manifestations of the Spirit. From a minister's perspective, there is a point where you become comfortable with ministering the message. A *preacher* primarily *proclaims* the gospel. A *teacher,* however, *explains* the gospel. But ministers sometimes become so comfortable delivering their messages that they can fall into a habit of not allowing the Holy Spirit an opportunity to manifest the spiritual gifts. I think ministers should always give the Holy Spirit an opportunity to move in the service, even if it means shortening the message. It takes faith to step out and minister in the Spirit. This can initially feel uncomfortable if a minister is not used to doing this. But it soon becomes pleasant; and giving the Holy Spirit the opportunity to move will add a new depth to one's ministry.

The manifestation of the Spirit is for the profit of all. It profits the one who is operating in the gift, and it profits the person who is on the receiving end of the gift. The receiver may be one person or vast numbers of people. The gifts are for our profit. They are not for our failure. The gifts of the Spirit will produce untold blessing in your life and in the lives of others.

If you like to profit, then you will be thrilled by the manifestations of the Spirit. The Greek word "profit" means "profitable, useful, expedient, and to be an advantage." God wants you to have an advantage in life. God wants you to profit. The Holy Spirit wants you to experience victory in all walks of your life. As we now begin to study each individual gift, allow the Spirit to come forth in a fresh and new way in your faith.

3

The Most Excellent Gift of the Word of Wisdom

But the manifestation of the Spirit is given to each one for the profit of all: for to one is given the word of wisdom through the Spirit... (1 Corinthians 12:7-8).

In the book of First Corinthians in the twelfth chapter, the apostle Paul shares with us the gifts of the Holy Spirit. Nine gifts are mentioned and they are all supernatural. I would like us to look at the gift of the *word of wisdom.* This gift is often misspoken as being the "gift of wisdom." But wisdom to have good success in life is different from the supernatural word of wisdom. God gave unto Solomon natural wisdom so that he could wisely govern the nation of Israel. Solomon's wisdom caused peace and prosperity to flourish in Israel as he continually made wise choices based upon good biblical principles. We are told in the book of James that if we lack wisdom then we are to ask God who will give it to us generously. We are also told in the book of Proverbs that wisdom is the most precious thing to possess in the entire world. Natural wisdom is not, however, a spiritual gift. Let me share an example to demonstrate this.

Let's say you want to buy a new car; you therefore use natural wisdom to shop around to find the best deal. You go to a car dealership to see the car you are interested in. The first dealership you visit does not have in stock the particular color of the car you desire. The salesperson is rude and you are not treated with courtesy. They do not offer you a decent trade-in on your used car, and they refuse to sell you the car at the price for which you would like to negotiate. No mention is made of any rebates on their vehicles, nor is any personal interest shown in you as a potential long-term customer. Eventually you leave the first dealership feeling unappreciated, and then drive across town to the second dealership.

As soon as you walk onto the grounds of this dealership you are courteously greeted by a salesperson who not only wants to sell you a car but is genuinely interested in making you a well-satisfied customer. Upon entering the showroom, you immediately see the car you desire on display and in the exact color you want. The atmosphere of the dealership is pleasant and comfortable and you are made to feel of value. As you negotiate the price of the car, the sales staff offers to bring you a drink and some small snacks, and they are willing to gladly stay late to work out a fair and respectable deal for you. They offer to give you an excellent trade-in value for your used car, and they also reveal that there is a rebate they can offer you from the manufacturer on the new car that will lower your cost by $2,500. They meet the price range you feel comfortable with and offer you a square deal.

So, where do you buy your car—from the first dealership or the second? Obviously the wise choice would be from the second dealership. In order to reach this decision is it necessary for God to give you a word of wisdom, or can you simply use natural wisdom to see that the second dealership would be the best choice? There is a difference between natural wisdom and the supernatural word of wisdom.

In the mind of God is contained all wisdom. Through the Holy Spirit a word of wisdom can be shared with a believer that reveals supernatural wisdom. The word of wisdom will always be future tense. It will speak regarding something you are to do, or reveal something that is going to happen. Hidden things are revealed that we would not normally know. In essence, the word of wisdom is the revealing of supernatural instruction, direction, or guidance that reveals the perfect will of God concerning a specific situation.

The word of wisdom is one of the three revelation gifts. The other two are "word of knowledge" and "discerning of spirits." They are called revelation gifts because they reveal something that is beyond our natural ability to know. The word of wisdom often operates in the prophet's ministry because the prophet preaches the Word; and as he does, he reveals the will of God. You see this gift manifested throughout the Bible. All nine gifts of the Holy Spirit were in operation in the Old Testament, except for tongues and the interpretation of tongues. Today we have all nine in manifestation in the Lord's church as the Holy Spirit leads.

ELISHA AND THE WORD OF WISDOM

Elisha worked many miracles by the power of the Holy Spirit. As a prophet his life was yielded to God thus allowing the Lord to accomplish much through him. One time, Elisha was approached by a woman in great need. She said to him, "Your servant my husband is dead, and you know that your servant feared the Lord. And the creditor is coming to take my two sons to be his slaves." So Elisha said to her, "What shall I do for you? Tell me, what do you have in the house?" And she said, "Your maidservant has nothing in the house but a jar of oil" (see 2 Kings 4:1-2).

Here we see the tragic result caused by bad financial decisions. This woman's husband was a prophet and loved God. It is possible to love the Lord, go to church, pray, and still have a financial mess in your life. Christians are not exempt from making bad choices with their money. The debt collectors don't care if you go to church or sing in the choir; they simply want the money that is due them. The husband died leaving the wife with a mountain of debt. It wouldn't surprise me a single bit if the financial problems he was experiencing contributed to this man's early death. Financial pressure is proven to cause numerous health-related problems such as high blood pressure, ulcers, depression, digestive problems, and other negative health effects. High levels of financial anxiety can even lead to a heart attack. Money problems are also one of the leading contributors to the erosion of a marriage, in some cases even leading to divorce.

The man dies and his wife now inherits the responsibility of the debt he left behind. The woman tells Elisha of her problem and he responds by saying, "What shall I do for you?" He basically was letting her know that the problem is beyond his natural ability to handle. It is not reasonable for Elisha to be expected to go around using his personal money to fix the financial problems of others. Even wealthy people would soon be depleted of their fortunes if they gave to every person who asked for help. Elisha implies by his response that perhaps he would help if he had sufficient funds, but the debt was most likely beyond his ability to pay. The good news is that God is not limited. He has an infinite supply of resources that will never run out. When we put our trust in God, He will make a way of deliverance for us.

Suddenly the Holy Spirit moves upon Elisha and he is prompted to ask the woman what thing of value she has in her house. Her response is that she has a small jar of oil. The success of Elisha's ministry depended upon the help of the Holy Spirit. The Holy Spirit now directs Elisha to tell the indebted woman to do something unusual.

When you are in a desperate place and your back is against the wall, you are usually more likely to obey a directive from God even if it stretches your understanding. In a crisis situation people discover that desperate times call for desperate measures. God can work through our most difficult experiences to bring us into a deeper understanding of His wondrous ways.

Elisha speaks to the woman a word of wisdom: "Go, borrow vessels from everywhere, from all your neighbors—empty vessels; do not gather just a few. And when you have come in, you shall shut the door behind you and your sons; then pour it into all those vessels, and set aside the full ones" (2 Kings 4:3-4). The instruction is to tell a woman drowning in debt to go and further borrow something that she doesn't own. From a natural perspective it appears to be foolish, but from a spiritual perspective it is her way of escape.

God has all wisdom within Himself, and He can send you just what you need to move forward. You may feel like you are stuck between a rock and a hard place, but God can still get you out. Here we see an example of supernatural wisdom. It may literally be a single word, or it could be a few short sentences as we see here in this example with Elisha. But it is not normal, everyday-type wisdom. It is supernatural, and it is very brief and to the point. One little word from God is all you need. When obeyed, it will always work—guaranteed.

This widowed woman begins to pour oil from her jar and it miraculously flowed until every jar was filled. When all the jars were filled, the oil stopped flowing. Often when the gifts of the Spirit are in operation you will see several gifts dovetail together. The flowing of the oil was in the category of "working of miracles." The word of wisdom and the "working of miracles" were both manifested by the Holy Spirit. These gifts are still manifested in the church today by simply being open to embracing the ministry of the Holy Spirit.

When you think of the flowing oil, you can't help but think about God's inexhaustible supply. Elisha instructs the woman to sell the oil, pay off her debt, and use the remaining funds to live on. God is so good that He doesn't stop by providing enough to only pay off the debt, but also giving abundance so that the woman and her two sons can live comfortably. Thank God for the Holy Spirit. Thank God for His gifts that are manifested in His people.

When the word of wisdom comes, you must simply obey what the Holy Spirit leads you to do. You would be surprised at what the Holy Spirit can say at times. Always remember, the manifestation of the Spirit is for your "profit." In other words, whatever He tells you to do is in the direction of making your life sweeter.

TIMING

One time, I was in my bathroom at home, standing in front of the mirror at the sink. While shaving, I heard the Holy Spirit speak to me so clearly that it sounded as if someone spoke in an audible voice. The Holy Spirit said, "Take off the Timex watch you are wearing, I am going to give you a Rolex watch." When I heard this I couldn't help but laugh a little bit, knowing that an upgrade to a Rolex would certainly be nicer than my three-year-old banged-up Timex with its cracked rubber strap.

Two weeks later, I was in Asia speaking in a conference and there was a strong presence of the Lord as I ministered. When I finished speaking I went and sat down, but the glory of the Lord was still hovering over the people. Without any doing of my own, people began to walk forward and lay money at my feet. I did not minister on the subject of finances, but I spoke about the ministry of the angels. The Holy Spirit was moving the hearts of the people to give as He was leading them.

One particular man walked over from his chair, handed me some money, then he went back to his seat and sat down. I couldn't help but notice that when he sat down he appeared to be having some sort of dispute with an invisible person. This man lifted his hands in an effort to display resistance, he grabbed his own head as if he were trying to cover his hears to not hear what was being spoken to him. The scene was actually somewhat comical looking. Suddenly he got up from his seat, walked over to me again while removing his watch from his wrist, placed it within my hands, and said, "This is for you." I looked and saw that he had given me a Rolex watch. It was a new model that was designed to be worn by international travelers, allowing a person to view the local time as well as multiple time zones simultaneously. The watch was a good fit to aide me in my call of spreading the gospel through world travel and ever-changing time zones.

The next day I saw the man who gave me his watch and I had a few minutes to talk with him. I was curious to know why he was making all of those expressions of resistance while he was sitting in his chair. In his own words this is what he said:

> After you finished ministering yesterday, I heard the Holy Spirit speak to me and say, "Give Steven Brooks your Rolex watch." Upon hearing this, I walked over to you and handed you some money. When I returned to my seat the Holy Spirit spoke again, saying, "I did not tell you to give him money, I told you to give him your Rolex." As I sat in my chair I endeavored to disregard His statement. I argued with God, I covered my head, I swung my arms in an effort to resist, but the more I resisted the more loudly He spoke, until I realized that I must obey God. It was then that I walked over to you and gave you my watch.

The Lord has a sense of humor. When God wants to bless you, there is no power in the universe that can inhibit Him. When the conference had concluded, I had some time to relax with the conference host. As we talked together I shared with him about how God spoke to me before this trip and told me, while shaving in the bathroom, to remove my Timex watch so that I might receive a Rolex watch. Then I showed him the watch I was given during the conference. The conference host joyfully laughed and said recently he was at his home in the bathroom shaving when he distinctly heard the Holy Spirit say to him, "Take off your Seiko watch, I am going to give you a Rolex watch." In obedience to God he took off his watch and shortly thereafter someone unexpectedly gave him a Rolex watch. He was wearing the watch which he had been given, so he showed it to me. It was a beautiful model.

The word of wisdom must be acted upon. This minister and me are not ones who are "money-minded," rather we pursue the Lord and simply aim to obey the Lord in all areas of our lives. As you walk before the Lord in obedience to His Word you will see the blessings of God enter every dimension of your life.

> By humility and the fear of the Lord are riches and honor
> and life (Proverbs 22:4).

When the word of wisdom comes, you simply obey, even if it is something as unusual as taking a watch. It is my conviction that if my friend and I never took off our old watches in obedience to God's directive, then we would not have received the intended blessing of the Lord. Two years went by and I ministered again in Asia at the same place where I had gone before. While there, I again saw the same man who gave his watch to me. He greeted me and kindly asked if he could see the watch he had previously given to me. Since I happened to be wearing it, I rolled up my shirtsleeve and showed it to him. Upon seeing it he smiled and said, "I have wondered which watch it was that I gave to you. At home I have a large collection of watches and I couldn't remember which specific one I gave away. Thank you for letting me see which one it was." Later on his daughter told me that he has a large collection of luxury watches. I felt the Lord allowed me to know this because God is a God of abundance and it made me feel good knowing this Christian friend wasn't going around without a watch. God always has more than enough. It makes me happy to know this man is blessed with so many watches.

The man with the large collection of watches reminds me of a local man who owns a huge amount of land in the county in which I live. One of the deacons in my church knows this man and he told me a funny but true story regarding him. One day this man was driving around and he saw a beautiful piece of land that really caught his eye. He stopped his car and said to his assistant, "Find out who owns that land because I want to buy it." The next day the assistant told the man, "I found out who owns the land, but you can't buy it." "Why not?" replied the man. The assistant said, "Because the owner is you!" The reality was that this man owned so much land that he couldn't remember all of the properties that were his. It's important to know that there is always someone out there who has the ability to bless you because they have more than they need.

A CLASSIC EXAMPLE

You have to be determined to obey the Lord regardless of what He says because there are times in which His directives may not make a lot of natural sense. No better example of this can be found than in Matthew's Gospel. Out of all the examples in the Bible that display the word of wisdom, this is my favorite because it is a classic example of our need to obey the Lord even when it does not appear logical to do so. Our story is found in Matthew chapter 17.

When they had come to Capernaum those who received the temple tax came to Peter and said, "Does your Teacher not pay the temple tax?" He said, "Yes." And when he had come into the house, Jesus anticipated him, saying, "What do you think, Simon? From whom do the kings of the earth take customs or taxes, from their sons or from strangers?" Peter said to Him, "From strangers." Jesus said to him, "Then the sons are free. Nevertheless, lest we offend them, go to the sea, cast in a hook, and take the fish that comes up first. And when you have opened its mouth, you will find a piece of money; take that and give it to them for Me and you" (Matthew 17:24-27).

When it comes to paying our taxes, I'm sure we can all relate to this story. Everyone today who is a working adult has to pay some form of tax. It was the same way during the time in which Jesus lived. All adult Jewish males were required to pay an annual tax of two drachmas to support the upkeep and maintenance of the Temple in Jerusalem. Two drachmas were equivalent to two days of wages. Rabbis were exempt from paying this tax and so were the priests in Jerusalem. Jesus tells Peter that from a technical standpoint the sons of the kingly rulers are exempt from taxes. Jesus is King of the Temple and He should not have to pay the tax. However, Jesus knew the religious leaders would not accept Him as the King of Israel, so He yielded His privileged right so not to offend those who were already looking for the slightest misstep to accuse Him. We need to be sensitive to honor other viewpoints as long as it does not require us to compromise our beliefs.

Jesus directs Peter to go on a fishing trip. Peter was formerly a professional fisherman before joining full-time ministry work with Jesus. He knew how to fish from a boat with a net. But Jesus instructs him to simply lower a hook into the water (with no bait on the hook) and to pull up the first fish he catches. Peter has now been around the Lord long enough to know that it is just best to go ahead and do exactly what He tells him to do even if it seems unusual. Peter could easily remember the instance three years earlier when he fished all night and caught nothing. After cleaning his nets and neatly putting everything away, Jesus came along and told Peter to launch his boat out into the deep for a catch. The enormous catch that he hauled in that day made an unforgettable impression upon Peter's mind. He had seen the Lord's words come to pass over and over again. So, he grabs a line and a hook and goes down to the beach. Have you ever gone fishing before to pay your taxes?

Peter drops a line into the water with a hook and quickly snags a fish. He opens its mouth and finds a Roman coin (double drachma) that is the exact amount needed to pay the Temple tax for two people. He obeys the Lord and pays the Lord's tax first, and then he happily pays his.

This is a marvelous demonstration of the word of wisdom coming forth to meet a need through a supernatural way. Normally you would never think of paying your tax bill by going fishing. It was the mighty Holy Spirit who revealed to Jesus the word of wisdom. Jesus shared the word with Peter and it worked. The same Holy Spirit is able to speak to you just as He spoke to Jesus. He can also give you a word of wisdom that speaks toward a situation you must deal with, or He can give you a word of wisdom to share with a loved one, or even to a complete stranger.

The word of wisdom will only work for that specific situation. In other words, Jesus told Peter to go fishing and pull up a fish with a coin in its mouth to pay both of their taxes. But you and I can't go out and duplicate the same act of fishing and expect it to work for us with the same results. You can't take someone else's word of wisdom and apply it to your life, unless the Lord also speaks the same thing to you. Understanding how this gift operates would clear up some unpleasant experiences that people needlessly suffer. When the word of wisdom truly originates from God, you will experience its full blessing. If the "word" is fabricated from within the soul of a person and is not initiated by the Holy Spirit, that person will experience unnecessary failure.

DISCERNMENT

For example, a minister who taught at a Bible college shared how the Lord spoke to a specific young man attending the college and instructed him to give away his used car to a certain person who did not have an automobile. The student who gave his car away shared a remarkable testimony three days later and told how someone unexpectedly gave him a brand new car. Well, when the other Bible college students heard this, it created a lot of excitement. There were several students who then gave their vehicles away for free—and ended up having to walk for the remainder of the semester. They tried to copy the one student's experience, but you must learn to discern whether or not God has spoken the same thing to you.

The prophet Elisha told Naaman to wash in the Jordan River seven times so that he might be clean of his leprosy. If you have leprosy today, you may go to the same river and wash seven times but you will not be healed *unless* God specifically told you through a word of wisdom to do that. To properly interpret God's Word, we should not take events or stories out of context and then endeavor to build doctrines that are based from an incorrect way of viewing Scripture. A good example of this can be found in the Gospel of Mark concerning the story of the rich young ruler.

> *Now as He was going out on the road, one came running,*
> *knelt before Him, and asked Him, "Good Teacher, what*

shall I do that I may inherit eternal life?" So Jesus said to him, "Why do you call Me good? No one is good but One, that is, God. You know the commandments: 'Do not commit adultery,' 'Do not murder,' 'Do not steal,' 'Do not bear false witness,' 'Do not defraud,' 'Honor your father and your mother.'" And he answered and said to Him, "Teacher, all these things I have kept from my youth" (Mark 10:17-20).

This young man approaches Jesus with sincere spiritual hunger. The Lord covers familiar ground to assess the young man's obedience to the basic requirements of keeping God's commandments. By the anointing of the Holy Spirit, Jesus ministers to the requests of this young man in a very personal way. With love, Jesus looked at the young man and said, "One thing you lack." There was one thing that was blocking this man from further spiritual progress—the reality that he trusted in his riches. This "one thing" is actually a "word of knowledge" in manifestation. There could possibly have been a hundred things blocking this man's path to God, but the Holy Spirit revealed to Jesus through the "word of knowledge" (which we will study in the next chapter) that his trust in riches was the only thing holding him back.

Now that the hindrance has been brought to light, Jesus addresses the man with a word of wisdom. The word of wisdom is the supernatural instruction from God that solves the problem and reveals the way to move forward.

"Go your way, sell whatever you have and give to the poor, and you will have treasure in heaven; and come, take up the cross, and follow Me." But he was sad at this word, and went away sorrowful, for he had great possessions (Mark 10:21-22).

Sadly, this young man *did not* obey the word of wisdom. He stepped back from entering into the perfect will of God. When we disobey God and walk away from Him, we are left with an empty life that has no true purpose or meaning. But concerning the word of wisdom that Jesus had for that specific young man, you can't take that "word" and try to apply it to everyone else. It is very possible that the Lord may still speak a similar directive to some, but He is the one who chooses who to speak it to, not us.

NOTHING—EXCEPT GOD

The Lord once spoke to a young man named Francis through a dream when he was 25 years of age. The year was 1208. Francis was the son of a very wealthy cloth merchant from Assisi, Italy. For years he had lived the wild life, much to the despair of his parents. When the Lord spoke to Francis in the dream, it produced a remarkable salvation experience in his life. Francis lost his interest in his father's business and wanted to serve God. His father was furious and took him before a public town meeting and demanded that his son renounce his rights as an heir. At this point Francis stripped off his beautiful clothes, which his father had given him, till he had nothing on but a long, thin undershirt. He renounced all of his family's fortune and then he went off into the freezing woods—singing as he went. Shortly thereafter he was beaten by robbers who also took his undershirt. He crawled out of a ditch and went off singing again. Now he was truly left with nothing—except God.

After spending an entire night in prayer in a bold effort to seek the will of God for his life and ministry, Francis went to the church that morning at San Nicolo in the town square. There he randomly opened up his Bible to three places, trusting that the Holy Spirit would give him three Scriptures upon which he would base his method of living. The first Scripture he came to was the following verse:

> *Jesus said to him, "If you want to be perfect, go, sell what*
> *you have and give to the poor, and you will have treasure*
> *in heaven; and come, follow Me"* (Matthew 19:21).

The moment Francis read this verse he knew the word of wisdom was being spoken to him. The second verse which he opened to is found in the Gospel of Luke:

> *And He said to them, "Take nothing for the journey,*
> *neither staffs nor bag nor bread nor money; and do not*
> *have two tunics apiece* (Luke 9:3).

The third and final confirming Scripture was the clincher for Francis, confirming to him what would be his course for life. As he randomly opened the Scriptures and allowed his eyes to fall upon them, he saw:

> *Then He said to them all, "If anyone desires to come after*
> *Me, let him deny himself, and take up his cross daily, and*
> *follow Me* (Luke 9:23).

Francis accepted these three verses as being the supernatural word of wisdom that he needed from God. Francis' small group of two members soon grew to four members, and during his lifetime multiplied into an international group of deeply committed men and women who eventually became known as the Order of the Franciscans. By the time of his death in 1226 there were over 5,000 men and women living and working in every country in Europe who belonged to his Order. They came from all walks of life, some having left behind royalty and tremendous wealth in order to follow after God in a way they saw as being unhindered from the distractions of the world. Even today Saint Francis is one of the most well-known saints to have ever lived. He's still tremendously popular even though he died over 800 years ago. Part of the success of his ministry was doing specifically what God told him to do. He obeyed the supernatural word of wisdom regarding his life's calling.

God can give a word of wisdom to a person like Saint Francis instructing him to live an austere life similar to John the Baptist. He also can give the word of wisdom to others who may be completely in the opposite direction, such as His will for a person to become a high-ranking political official, or for one to establish and lead a multibillion-dollar corporation. You must follow the unique path that God has for your life. This is why the word of wisdom is priceless—it reveals to you God's will and plan for your life.

SPECIFIC WORD OF WISDOM

We see the word of wisdom coming forth to individuals through-out the Bible. The story of Isaac takes a specific turn for good in Genesis chapter 26.

> *There was a famine in the land, besides the first famine that was in the days of Abraham. And Isaac went to Abimelech king of the Philistines, in Gerar. Then the Lord appeared to him and said: "Do not go down to Egypt; live in the land of which I shall tell you. Dwell in this land, and I will be with you and bless you (Genesis 26:1-3).*

At a pivotal point in his life, we see that Isaac receives a word of wisdom just when he needs it most. The Lord appears to Isaac and tells him where he is to live. I have to speculate here, but I strongly suspect the reason the Lord appeared to Isaac is in order to answer his prayer for direction. At this time a famine is taking place. Isaac seeks to move south away from an area of drought and devastation and move to somewhere outside of the famine's cruel effects. Isaac was a godly man and surely would have sought the Lord in prayer to find out where to go.

Your prayer life plays a vital role in the manifestation of spiritual gifts. God answers prayer, and He gives Isaac specific instructions:

1. Do not go down into Egypt

2. Dwell in this land

3. I will be with you and bless you here

Isaac receives and obeys the word of wisdom because the Bible says, "So Isaac dwelt in Gerar" (verse 6). Gerar was a town in what is today south-central Israel. The word "gerar" in Hebrew means "sojourner." This was a temporary place for Isaac, but it was the perfect will of God for Isaac at this phase of his life. Because he is in the right place and has obeyed God, he is now positioned to be blessed. God is able to bless you regardless of outward circumstances that seem impossible to overcome.

> *Then Isaac sowed in that land, and reaped in the same year a hundredfold; and the Lord blessed him. The man began to prosper, and continued prospering until he became very prosperous* (Genesis 26:12-13).

Let us consider that Isaac is a wise man. He would not do something foolish that would cause harm or loss to him or his family. Yet the Bible tells us that he sowed seed in the land. Keep in mind that the land is experiencing a famine. No farmer with any kind of farming knowledge would sow during the middle of a famine. But that's exactly what Isaac did. Can you imagine what the Philistine neighbors must have thought? They watch from afar as Isaac breaks open the soil of the cracked and parched ground. As he sows seed into the ground, they probably laughed knowing that there was no water and no rain to be expected anytime soon. They very well could have thought that the scorching sun had a damaging effect on Isaac's mind. After all, from a natural perspective what he is doing does appear to be foolish. It appears as if he is throwing away good seed. Why did Isaac do this?

Although not mentioned in Scripture, I believe the reason Isaac sowed during a time of famine was because God told him to do it. Most likely, he received another word of wisdom that instructed him to carry out this daring act of faith. Did it work? We are told that within the same year Isaac reaped a hundredfold. The Apostle Paul told us that the spiritual gifts are for our profit. Isaac profited by obeying the word of wisdom. He stayed in Gerar and allowed the Lord to bless Him there.

Apostle Paul was also familiar with the manifestation of the word of wisdom. As Paul matured in his ministry he suffered much persecution. Violent mobs, riots, physical beatings, and all manner of hardships were in his path. While at Corinth, Paul testified to the Jews who lived there that Jesus is the Christ. His message was strongly opposed and the Jews even blasphemed. Yet Paul stays in Corinth despite the initial verbal hostility shown to him. In his mind perhaps he wondered when the next mob would form and show up where he was staying. He was most likely struggling to hold his peace and keep his mind on his ministry work. At this stage, we see the Lord Jesus appear to Paul and share with him a word of wisdom.

> *Now the Lord spoke to Paul in the night by a vision, "Do not be afraid, but speak, and do not keep silent; for I am with you, and no one will attack you to hurt you; for I have many people in this city." And he continued there a year and six months, teaching the word of God among them* (Acts 18:9-11).

The first thing the Lord told Paul was to not be afraid. This would imply that the great difficulties and discouragement that Paul was facing had caused him to drift over into fear. Jesus personally speaks to him in comforting words by then saying, "for I am with you." Knowing that the Lord is with you is a great source of strength and relief. The Lord also adds that, "no one will attack you to hurt you." On this statement Paul most likely breathed a big sigh of relief. Paul's body needed a break from the physical hardships. The Lord will never allow you to be tempted with more than you can bear. The Lord also informs Paul that He has many people in the city of Corinth. Notice that this supernatural word of wisdom is brief, concise, and reveals God's perfect will for Paul and his ministry work while in Corinth.

Paul stays in Corinth for a year and six months, teaching the word of God to the people. The Lord told Paul that everything would be okay, and all was well. There was a moment, however, when the devil stirred up trouble and it looked like Paul was in a real dilemma, possibly even in danger of his life.

> *When Gallio was proconsul of Achaia, the Jews with one accord rose up against Paul and brought him to the judgment seat, saying, "This fellow persuades men to worship God contrary to the law." And when Paul was about to open his mouth, Gallio said to the Jews, "If it were a matter of wrongdoing or wicked crimes, O Jews, there would be reason why I should bear with you. But if it is a question of words and names and your own law, look to it yourselves; for I do not want to be a judge of such matters." And he drove them from the judgment seat. Then all the Greeks took Sosthenes, the ruler of the synagogue, and beat him before the judgment seat. But Gallio took no notice of these things (Acts 18:12-17).*

Again we see that the word of wisdom, which Jesus earlier gave to Paul, proved true. Paul was never harmed just as he was told. When trouble came, God worked through a man to defend Paul. When it was all finished, the main instigator, Sosthenes, ended up getting the physical beating—not Paul. Later in the book of Acts we see Paul reveal another example of how the word of wisdom came to him.

> *"Now it happened, when I returned to Jerusalem and was praying in the temple, that I was in a trance and saw Him saying to me, 'Make haste and get out of Jerusalem quickly, for they will not receive your testimony concerning Me'"* (Acts 22:17-18).

Here we find Paul telling his Damascus road experience to a hostile group of Jews in Jerusalem. Paul recalls how earlier in his life he was in Jerusalem after the days of his salvation experience. He greatly desired to share the good news with the Jews, but Jesus appeared to Paul in a trance. Pau heard Him instruct him to leave immediately because his life was in physical danger. Paul was divinely told that the Jews would not receive his testimony. The Lord then concluded the word of wisdom with this closing statement:

> *Then He said to me, "Depart, for I will send you far from here to the Gentiles"* (Acts 22:21).

We have to rely upon the Holy Spirit to give us the word of wisdom. This gift in operation can actually save the lives of people. Jesus told Paul to make haste and get out of Jerusalem. When the word of wisdom comes, there is no time to debate with God. The Lord knows things that we are not aware of. We must cooperate with the Holy Spirit to walk in the fullness of His blessings.

READ THE BIBLE

The number one way that I often receive a word of wisdom is through reading my Bible. I couldn't even begin to recall all of the times when God has spoken to me through this method. It almost always happens when I am not expecting it. The experience is somewhat similar to what happened with Saint Francis when he randomly opened the Bible while trusting God that the pages would open to just the right spot. But for me this happens when God seems to catch me off guard, when I am not even thinking about receiving a word of wisdom.

For example, a few days ago I was putting my daughter to bed at about 10 o'clock at night. She had school the next morning so my intention was to immediately pray for her, turn out the lights and have her go to sleep. However, we ended up talking until about 10:45 P.M. We discussed the Bible and certain things that were on her mind about the Lord. Young people have a lot of questions about God. As parents we should take the time to explain spiritual things to our children. Some of these things we often take for granted because as adults we may already grasp them, but for young people they may be still learning it for the first time. That night we discussed the mystery of the Holy Trinity—how there are three separate Persons but still only one God.

After I put my daughter to sleep in her bed, I went downstairs to use the restroom before going to bed. In the restroom I quietly thanked the Lord for blessing me with my daughter and for the work of grace He has done in her heart. I said, "Lord, thank You for my daughter and that You are working in her life. Thank You, Jesus for the peace You have given us." Then I saw a Bible lying on the counter so I picked it up and randomly opened it. When I opened the Bible, the pages fell open upon the book of Isaiah and I saw a verse appear to lift up off the page in almost a three dimensional way. The verse was supernaturally highlighted to such a degree that I did not notice what was before it or after it. The verse said:

> *All your children shall be taught by the Lord, and great shall be the peace of your children* (Isaiah 54:13).

This verse took my breath away. The Holy Spirit is the voice of God. When the Holy Spirit gives you a word of wisdom, it is the very same thing as Jesus standing there in person and speaking it to you. Needless to say, I went to sleep that night with a smile on my face after seeing that verse spoken to me in such a personal way, knowing that my daughter is held in the hands of God. There are other ways in which a person can receive a word of wisdom. Angels can be sent by God to deliver a message. These messages often contain words of wisdom that are necessary for us to receive.

A word of wisdom can often contain a type of divine guidance. There is a difference between the inward guidance of the Holy Spirit and a manifestation of the word of wisdom. The most common method of guidance for the believer is through the "inward witness." This is seen in the following Scriptures:

> *For as many as are led by the Spirit of God, these are sons of God* (Romans 8:14).

> *The Spirit Himself bears witness with our spirit that we are children of God* (Romans 8:16).

How does a believer in Christ know they are saved? It is not determined by how a person feels. It is possible to wake up in the morning and due to a bad night of restless sleep, a person may not "feel" saved. But thank God we are still saved despite what our feelings tell us. As a child of God, you know you are saved because the Holy Spirit bears witness on the inside, within your spirit, that you are a child of God.

This is the number one way in which people know they have been born again in Christ. This constant inward confirmation that is given by the Holy Spirit not only reveals the genuine experience and security of your salvation, but it is also the primary method that God uses to lead you in other areas of your life. There are also other methods in which God may choose to lead you such as by giving you a word of wisdom. The word of wisdom will always be in agreement with the Bible, and it will peacefully harmonize with you inwardly.

ANGELIC DELIVERY

It is important to understand that at times God may choose to give you a word of wisdom through an angel. Whether it is an angel carrying a message or a donkey speaking to a prophet, these manifestations are brought forth by the Holy Spirit. We are never to seek after angels or try to force things to happen that only the Holy Spirit can bring forth. We should be content to allow the Lord to choose if He wants to grant us such an experience.

On the other hand, we don't want to shut out these divine workings because of a lack of understanding. It is wise to be open to the ministry of the angels because sometimes this is the method that God selects to have a word of wisdom given to us. The receiving of words of wisdom through angels may seem strange to some, but not to those who are familiar with their Bibles. There are many instances in the Bible where God has used holy angels to intervene in the lives of people and supply supernatural guidance through a word of wisdom. This happened to Joseph, the stepfather of Jesus, several times.

> *But while he thought about these things, behold, an angel of the Lord appeared to him in a dream, saying, "Joseph, son of David, do not be afraid to take to you Mary your wife, for that which is conceived in her is of the Holy*

Spirit. And she will bring forth a Son, and you shall call His name Jesus, for He will save His people from their sins" (Matthew 1:20-21).

Joseph received through an angel a word of wisdom concerning how he should treat Mary in light of the fact that she was pregnant and he was not the father of the baby. If I was in a perplexing situation like Joseph was in, I would also welcome a word of wisdom to gain insight of what to do. The angel also told Joseph the name for the child, which was to be Jesus. Joseph received words of wisdom through other instructions shared in further angel visits.

Now when they had departed, behold, an angel of the Lord appeared to Joseph in a dream, saying, "Arise, take the young Child and His mother, flee to Egypt, and stay there until I bring you word; for Herod will seek the young Child to destroy Him" (Matthew 2:13).

Joseph was always quick to do exactly what he was told by the angel. When the angel told him to leave and flee to Egypt, he did not waste a moment of time. He quickly packed their belongings and they left that very night. Herod had issued an official government death edict on all male children in Bethlehem and its districts for those of the age of two years and under. Here is another instance of acting quickly upon a word of wisdom, which should always be carried out swiftly—lives may depend upon it.

A believer in Christ may say, "Pastor Steven, I'm not really interested in messages from angels and all that 'spiritual stuff'; all I want is to see people saved and go to heaven." A proper understanding of the various ways in which words of wisdom can come to you will facilitate the harvest of souls in which the church is actively engaged. After all, the very first Gentile convert was led to salvation in Christ through a process that involved an angel sharing a word of wisdom. In the tenth chapter of the book of Acts we have the story of the salvation of Cornelius and his entire household. In a vision, an angel of God came to Cornelius and instructed him to do the following:

> *About the ninth hour of the day he saw clearly in a vision an angel of God coming in and saying to him, "Cornelius! Now send men to Joppa, and send for Simon whose surname is Peter. He is lodging with Simon, a tanner, whose house is by the sea. He will tell you what you must do"* (Acts 10:3,5-6).

Angels do not preach the gospel, for that assignment belongs to the people of God. But angels do actively partner with us in the labor for souls to hear and receive the gospel. Cornelius obeyed the word of wisdom and he sent three men to the port city of Joppa to inquire for the Apostle Peter to come. Upon hearing the invitation to minister the gospel, Peter agreed to come to Caesarea to meet Cornelius. When Peter preached to Cornelius and his household, the Holy Spirit fell upon all who heard the word. The unbelievers were saved, filled with the Holy Spirit, spoke in tongues, and were baptized. Thus the first non-Jewish believers were added to the church.

If you want to see souls saved, you will want to utilize every possible means that God makes available to the church. God may want to send an angel to you to share a word of wisdom that will aid in the effort to bring salvation to a lost soul or an entire town. In a similar way, we see that an angel was involved in initiating Philip's journey, which concluded in the salvation of the Ethiopian eunuch.

> *Now an angel of the Lord spoke to Philip, saying, "Arise and go toward the south along the road which goes down from Jerusalem to Gaza"* (Acts 8:26).

Philip receives the word of wisdom through an angel but he is not told the purpose of his journey. He begins traveling in faith expecting something good to happen. He eventually crosses the path of a high-ranking government official who is the treasurer for the queen of the Ethiopians. He hears him reading from Isaiah the prophet. At this point the Holy Spirit speaks to Philip.

> *Then the Spirit said to Philip, "Go near and overtake this chariot"* (Acts 8:29).

We must now ask ourselves an interesting question. We initially see that an angel spoke to Philip to launch him on his journey. Now the Holy Spirit speaks to Philip with further instruction. The question is, "How do you tell the difference between the voice of an angel and the voice of the Holy Spirit?" There must be a distinction because Philip identifies the source of the two different voices. Over time I have learned that when an angel has spoken to me the voice appears to come from "outside" myself. Often it will seem to come from over my shoulder, as if a person were standing behind me and spoke.

When the Holy Spirit speaks, the voice comes from "within" and vocalizes then outward, very similar to a theatre surround-sound system. The voice seems to surround you. Also, the voice of the Holy Spirit is much more authoritative as compared to an angel. The voice of the Holy Spirit instantly inspires unusual boldness when He speaks to you.

The result of Philip's obedience to the word of wisdom brought by the angel and the Holy Spirit's direct word of wisdom is that another soul is brought into the kingdom of God.

> *Now as they went down the road, they came to some water. And the eunuch said, "See, here is water. What hinders me from being baptized?" Then Philip said, "If you believe with all your heart, you may." And he*

answered and said, "I believe that Jesus Christ is the Son of God." So he commanded the chariot to stand still. And both Philip and the eunuch went down into the water, and he baptized him (Acts 8:36-38).

We must be open to the biblical examples of angels bringing words of wisdom to us. Words of wisdom can also come to you through other believers as they are moved upon by the Holy Spirit. Since it's possible that the Holy Spirit can cause a donkey to speak to a person, we really should not let our finite minds put God in a box as to what His limits are. It's important to mature spiritually so that we can discern the voice of God and the leading of the Holy Spirit.

The word of wisdom is coming to you. God wants to help you. He wants to move you forward in the right direction by giving you a word of wisdom. Be receptive to this word coming to you. It will reveal to you what you are to do. It will bring forth God's very best into your life. Rejoice, and thank God for this marvelous gift operating in your life.

4

THE SUPERNATURAL GIFT OF THE WORD OF KNOWLEDGE

*But the manifestation of the Spirit is given to each one
for the profit of all...to another the word of knowledge
through the same Spirit* (1 Corinthians 12:7-8).

As we continue to study the gifts of the Spirit mentioned in First Corinthians the twelfth chapter, we see the tremendous gift known as the *word of knowledge*. Keep in mind as we study the gifts of the Spirit that all nine gifts mentioned are supernatural. I have heard some people describe this gift as the "gift of knowledge." However, there is no such thing as a gift of knowledge. Natural knowledge is not what we would describe as a supernatural gift. Knowledge is the acquiring of information, facts, and truths through the process of study or investigation. For instance, you can gain knowledge about the subject of dinosaurs by going to museums and viewing and touching their fossilized bones. You can further your knowledge by going on the Internet and searching for more writings and images of dinosaurs.

We live in a time when we now have quick access to gain knowledge on just about any subject that we have an interest in. Knowledge is so accessible today that we don't even have to go to a physical university to acquire a degree. People can now complete their degree through online studies, acquiring the knowledge they need from the comfort of their home. This modern-day explosion of knowledge, which is available at our fingertips, is a sure sign that we are now living in the end times before the Lord's soon return.

> But you, Daniel, keep this prophecy a secret; seal up the book until the time of the end, when many will rush here and there, and knowledge will increase (Daniel 12:4 NLT).

Knowledge is essential for us to have in order to live a life that allows us to make the best decisions based on the specific information we have gathered. The word of knowledge that comes from God reveals to us facts and truths, but its source does not originate from a textbook or Internet search engine. The word of knowledge is not an encyclopedia of knowledge, but is rather short, concise, and to the point. Saul's father once lost his donkeys, so he sent his son and a helper to go find them and bring them back. While looking for the donkeys, Saul meets the prophet Samuel. Samuel speaks to Saul and gives us a good example of the supernatural gift of the word of knowledge in manifestation.

> But as for your donkeys that were lost three days ago, do not be anxious about them, for they have been found. And on whom is all the desire of Israel? Is it not on you and on all your father's house? (1 Samuel 9:20)

The Holy Spirit revealed supernatural knowledge to the prophet Samuel about Saul's life concerning the lost donkeys he was searching for. It was not complete and total knowledge. The word was specific and short. It did not encompass an overview of Saul's entire life. It was not a book of knowledge, it was a word of knowledge. Samuel did not receive this knowledge from a news report on the television or through a text on his smartphone. The knowledge came to him supernaturally by the Holy Spirit. The revelation that the word of knowledge brings is always present tense or will speak to something that happened in the past.

God has within His awesome mind the sum total of all knowledge that exists within this universe as well as all dimensions of time and space. He is able to take a word of that knowledge and share it with us by the Holy Spirit. The word of knowledge works in such a unique way that it creates open doors for further ministry by the Spirit. As the word of knowledge is ministered, the hearts of the recipients are captured by an awareness of God's love for them. It's as if the word of knowledge disarms people from any preconceived fears they may have. This gift allows a person to let his or her guard down, allowing a deeper level of ministry by the Holy Spirit to operate.

Over the years I have seen the word of knowledge act as a breakthrough gift in my ministry that gives favor and then allows me to continue ministering more deeply to the person's needs. Two other ministers come to mind who were highly developed in this gift: Evangelist Kathryn Kuhlman and Prophet William Branham. The word of knowledge would operate through them and they would receive supernatural information about particular people. Prophet Branham would often receive from the Holy Spirit the name or the home street address of the person to whom he was ministering. The word of knowledge would be joyfully received by the recipient, and then the healing gifts which he and Ms. Kuhlman operated in would flow easily into that person.

Back to Saul and the donkeys. Once Saul knew that the lost donkeys were found, he then received prophetic ministry from the prophet Samuel, as the gift of prophesy came forth and Samuel spoke to Saul regarding his call to be king over Israel. Often the gifts of the Holy Spirit operate in tandem, thus working together to accomplish the will of God. I encourage you to be open to allowing multiple gifts to flow through you as well. The Holy Spirit will cause the gifts to flow through you in order to bring comfort to those in need and minister divine help just when it is needed most.

The gifts of the Spirit were in consistent manifestation in the life of our Lord Jesus. When you read through the four Gospels, you see them popping out over and over again. One of the best examples is found in Luke's Gospel, which we will see also contains reflections of divine humor and the willingness of Jesus to follow the spontaneous leading of the Holy Spirit.

> *Then Jesus entered and passed through Jericho. Now behold, there was a man named Zacchaeus who was a chief tax collector, and he was rich. And he sought to see who Jesus was, but could not because of the crowd, for he was of short stature. So he ran ahead and climbed up into a sycamore tree to see Him, for He was going to pass that way. And when Jesus came to the place, He looked up and saw him, and said to him, "Zacchaeus, make haste and come down, for today I must stay at your house"* (Luke 19:1-5).

Zacchaeus wanted to see what Jesus looked like. He had never seen Jesus before and Jesus had never met Zacchaeus before either. That is why he climbed the tree—to see Jesus. You don't climb a tree to see someone you have already seen. The two were complete strangers to each other. Thousands would often gather to see the "miracle worker" when He came into a town, so it was not always possible to get near Him because of the large crowds. Zacchaeus was short but he was smart and determined, so he anticipated the direction where Jesus was going and ran ahead of the crowd, climbed up a tree, and waited for Jesus to come by.

This story also tells us that Zacchaeus was a rich man. His actions to see Jesus give us a prophetic glimpse into why some people attain wealth and others do not. Many people are afraid to leave the crowd. They choose to follow the "herd mentality" and simply do what others suggest without asking any questions. I've seen this countless times at airports. People will stand in long lines simply because that is where everyone else is standing. Some don't even check to see if it's the correct line they are supposed to be in. They wait in line forty minutes to reach their terminal gate only to find out it was a line going to the restroom. Zacchaeus broke away from the crowd and got himself into an elevated position to see the Lord.

Rich people endeavor to position themselves by getting into the best position before the "next big thing" shows up. They climb high to see what the crowd is not aware of. Their effort pays off with the best view of where to invest their stock, where to place their retirement fund, and to anticipate which way the market is going before it ever gets there. They want to be in a favorable position so they are willing to take a risk by going "out on a limb."

Some Christians want a "risk-free" guarantee before they invest. They want someone else to climb the tree first and see if the branches can support their weight. But the rewards go to the risk takers who wisely balance the risk/reward ratio and step out on those rare opportunities that are presented. Zacchaeus took the risk of climbing the tree and the recompense of his faith included his salvation as well as his bold actions being recorded in the eternal word of God.

As Jesus comes by the tree, He sees Zacchaeus, and the first thing He says is, "Zacchaeus." This must have greatly startled Zacchaeus because he must have immediately thought within himself, *How does He know my name?* We must ask ourselves the same question. How did Jesus know the name of a total stranger? Zacchaeus has never met Jesus before; he doesn't even know what Jesus looks like. The Holy Spirit revealed to Jesus that the man's name up in the tree was Zacchaeus. This is the word of knowledge in operation. This wonderful gift has an amazing ability to grab a person's attention.

Every one of us enjoys being called by our name. Studies in psychology have revealed that the favorite thing we like to hear is our own name. Zacchaeus must have been deeply touched in his heart that Jesus was reaching out to him in such a personal way. I'm glad he didn't fall out of the tree in his excitement!

But the Holy Spirit has given to Jesus more insight than just the name of Zacchaeus. He continues saying, "Hurry and come down, for today I must stay at your house." Here we see the word of wisdom brought forth by the Holy Spirit. This is a supernatural gift.

For a modern-day example, what would you think if a complete stranger approached you and said, "I have twelve hungry men with me, and I and the men with me are coming to your house so you can serve all of us a meal." Perhaps you would respond by saying, "Well, I don't even know who you are. I do not feel comfortable allowing strangers into my home, and I certainly don't want to cook for all these men." But Jesus is operating in the Prophet's ministry. When the word of wisdom is received and obeyed, it will always bring about the result intended by God. Zacchaeus gladly responds to the Lord's directive; and as a result, salvation comes to Zacchaeus and to those in his house.

> *Then Zacchaeus stood and said to the Lord, "Look, Lord, I give half of my goods to the poor; and if I have taken anything from anyone by false accusation, I restore four-fold." And Jesus said to him, "Today salvation has come*

to this house, because he also is a son of Abraham; for the Son of Man has come to seek and to save that which was lost" (Luke 19:8-10).

From the example of Zaccheus we see how two of the gifts of the Spirit came forth to touch the lives of this Jewish family. Often the gifts operate in a way in which they are bundled together. This is why you should ask the Heavenly Father for all nine gifts to be manifested in your life. Allow yourself to be fluent in the spiritual gifts.

PERSONAL EXPERIENCES

The word of knowledge operates often in my life, especially when I am praying for the sick. When I place my hands on a sick person, it often feels like the Holy Spirit is doing a rapid scan of the person's spiritual and physical condition and relaying that knowledge to me. If the sickness is due to the presence of an evil spirit, then I will address that in my prayer for the person by rebuking the unclean spirit. If an evil spirit is not present, then it is simply a physical condition that needs healing. The Holy Spirit often reveals to me if a person is harboring unforgiveness toward someone and therefore not able to receive the healing anointing. Walking in unforgiveness will block the anointing of God, and a believer needs to forgive any offense in order to receive the Lord's healing power.

The word of knowledge usually comes forth at least one time for me every day and sometimes much more on days when I am ministering. One place this gift can really get activated is in prayer meetings with other Spirit-filled believers. Often at our church, when we pray in our corporate prayer meetings, we eventually reach a place where the Spirit moves freely among us. When this happens we all supernaturally know the subject area in which we are to focus our prayers.

For instance, I might feel led by the Spirit that we are to pray for the oil and gas sector of Israel's economy. Before I even start praying for this, the other intercessors have already found themselves thinking about the very same thing. Once finished with that area of prayer another intercessor may begin to pray for our president; and just before she starts praying for him, each of us in the room has begun thinking about our president. We move in the unison of the Spirit through the word of knowledge. We could literally finish each other's sentences because the Holy Spirit is sharing with our prayer group the same knowledge.

On certain days when I have more time to spend in prayer, I will move into a place where the word of knowledge becomes very pronounced in manifestation. When this happens the Holy Spirit will reveal things to me before they happen. Even small things He will share. Often the Holy Spirit will alert me that my phone is about to ring. Ten seconds after He shares this with me, my phone will ring with an incoming call. The Holy Spirit does this because sometimes I get so focused in prayer that I feel as if I have escaped to a peaceful retreat far away from the cares and problems of life. The peace and tranquility will be so wonderful that the Holy Spirit will tell me that my phone is about to ring so that I will not be startled out of this blissful state by the piercing ring of my cell phone.

Other times the Holy Spirit will share supernatural knowledge that touches even recreational situations. A few years ago I was in the bathroom praying because it was the quietest place in the house. After a few hours in prayer, the Holy Spirit gave me a word of knowledge and said, "Your wife and daughter will have fun exercising on the new Nintendo Wii." Of course, when the Holy Spirit said that I knew we did not have a Nintendo Wii. I stepped out of the bathroom and saw my wife coming down the hallway of our home. I said to Kelly, "You and Abigail will have fun exercising on the new Nintendo Wii."

With a surprised look she said, "How did you know that? Did you hear me talking on the phone a few minutes ago?" I replied by letting her know it was the Holy Spirit who told me this. She responded by saying she had just gotten off the phone and had ordered a new Nintendo Wii with the additional electronic stepping board designed for exercise use. A few days later it was delivered to our home and they were working up a sweat and having a great time together.

You may be surprised at what the Holy Spirit may share with you. It doesn't all have to be required or necessary information. The closer you get to the Lord, the more you will see that He wants to be your friend and He will speak freely with you about many things. When the word of knowledge comes to you, it is very easy to discern. It seems to just float into your mind as if a person were sitting next to you and said something to you.

RELY ON THE HOLY SPIRIT

In the Gospel of John we see the beautiful story of the woman at the well in the region of Samaria. Jesus is alone at the well when the woman arrives to get water. They have a brief conversation, and it is important to observe how Jesus would rely upon the Holy Spirit to help minister to the unsaved. Our natural conversations intended to lead the lost to Christ often only reach a place where we verbally spar or clash on religious differences that either side is unwilling to budge on. Jesus was dependent on the Holy Spirit to go beyond natural barriers that exist between the lost and the saved.

I learned many years ago that I cannot bring the lost to Christ through debates or well-crafted arguments. The preaching of the gospel of the kingdom must be carried out by the power of the Spirit with the gifts of the Spirit in manifestation. From a natural or mental perspective the conversation had gone about as far as it could go without being bogged down in cultural and religious differences. The

Holy Spirit would help Jesus move into the spiritual level to jump the boundaries that people hold to guard their cherished positions and beliefs.

> *The woman said to Him, "Sir, give me this water, that I may not thirst, nor come here to draw." Jesus said to her, "Go, call your husband, and come here." The woman answered and said, "I have no husband." Jesus said to her, "You have well said, 'I have no husband,' for you have had five husbands, and the one whom you now have is not your husband; in that you spoke truly." The woman said to Him, "Sir, I perceive that You are a prophet"* (John 4:15-19).

From the moment Jesus ministers to the woman in the power of the Spirit, the conversation takes a different turn. Some have described this method of ministry as "power evangelism" or "prophetic evangelism." I believe both of these descriptions are accurate; but if we look closely, we will see more clearly what specific spiritual gift was in operation when Jesus spoke to the woman at the well. How did Jesus know the woman was not married and that she had been previously married five times and that the man she was now living with was someone she was not married to? If we describe this as "prophetic evangelism," then what spiritual gift is being used? The gift that was operating through Jesus in this instance was without a doubt the word of knowledge. The Holy Spirit revealed to Jesus certain facts about this woman's condition.

I believe there are some people who are so difficult to reach that without the help of the Holy Spirit they will be lost. This woman has had certain life experiences that would imply she was not open to the gospel message. She is at the well alone, which is out of place because normally all the women go early in the morning to obtain their water. This was a social gathering that the women looked forward to in order to exchange fellowship, friendship, and most likely the latest gossip circulating through the town. She is alone and at the well during an odd time because she has been rejected by the village women. The local women want no relationship with her, perhaps because they are fearful she may try to entice their own husbands toward sin. She has been married five times. I would have to suspect that for men to still pursue her after multiple failed marriages, she must have been very physically attractive.

It was a divine assignment for this woman to meet and talk with Jesus. It was a once in a lifetime event. Jesus was able to break through to her because of the Holy Spirit who gave Him a word of knowledge just when it was most needed. Of course, you know the rest of the story has a marvelous outcome.

> *The woman then left her waterpot, went her way into the city, and said to the men, "Come, see a Man who told me all things that I ever did. Could this be the Christ?" Then they went out of the city and came to Him* (John 4:28-30).

It appears there was likely much more that Jesus revealed to this woman as He ministered to her as indicated from the phrase, "Come, see a Man who told me all things that I ever did." The Gospel of John only records a few things Jesus shared by the word of knowledge, but there was likely much more that He shared that was not recorded. The outcome of this one-on-one ministry is that it produced a spiritual harvest of many souls in the Samaritan village.

> *Then they said to the woman, "Now we believe, not because of what you said, for we ourselves have heard Him and we know that this is indeed the Christ, the Savior of the world"* (John 4:42).

When the church endeavors to win the lost for Christ but does not rely upon the Holy Spirit to aid in this vital work, then the efforts will return results that are only a small fraction of what God intends. Jesus is our greatest example, more so than Paul or Peter or any other minister. If Jesus was dependent upon the Holy Spirit to flow through Him and supply the needed spiritual gifts, then how much more do we also need to rely upon the Holy Spirit's power? In the context of ministering to the woman at the well and eventually to the Samaritan community at large, Jesus made the following statement. These words also apply to the global harvest that in our present age we are assigned to reach.

> *Do you not say, "There are still four months and then comes the harvest"? Behold, I say to you, lift up your eyes and look at the fields, for they are already white for harvest!* (John 4:35)

The gospel of the kingdom was always intended to be demonstrated, not just talked about. Signs, wonders, miracles, and the spiritual gifts are needed in order to bring the full gospel message to the lost. When the spiritual gifts are excluded, we are only preaching a half gospel. The word of knowledge was brought forth by the Holy Spirit to help Jesus break through the initial outward walls of resistance of the Samaritan woman.

The gifts are manifested to reach the lost and to also bless the people of God. Recently while in a meeting in which I was ministering, I had the Holy Spirit interrupt my sermon and share with me that He wanted to release a birthday blessing upon those who either had a birthday on that specific day, or the day before, or the day after. I asked for those individuals with birthdays within that time frame to come forward and three women responded. One woman's birthday was that day, the second woman's birthday was the day before, and the third woman's birthday was the next day. I had never met these three women before in my life. The Holy Spirit had me sing a song over them, which came to me prophetically. The song was basically about cruising on a ship and experiencing the love of God on a cruise ship. They begin to weep as I sang this funny song about God blessing them through a cruise on a ship.

After the meeting was over, the three ladies told me that they were very close friends and their friendship began twenty years earlier when all three of them met each other for the first time while on a cruise ship!

The Holy Spirit knows what He is doing. Let your spiritual ears be tuned to the voice of God. Allow your heart to be at peace and undisturbed so that you are sensitive to the Holy Spirit. The gift of the word of knowledge will surely flow through you.

5

THE MYSTERIOUS GIFT OF DISCERNING OF SPIRITS

But the manifestation of the Spirit is given to each one for the profit of all; for to one is given the... discerning of spirits... (1 Corinthians 12:7-8,10).

Many years back I began to study in earnest the gifts of the Holy Spirit. As I would read through them I was always intrigued by one particular gift. My curiosity was drawn to this gift primarily because I had no clue in the world what it was. The gift I am speaking of is the gift known in God's Word as *discerning of spirits.* My lack of understanding regarding this gift caused me to study it with a special emphasis. Once I began to understand what this gift actually was and how it operated, I begin to have an increase of its manifestation in my ministry. Before we look at what this gift is, let's first look at what it is not.

Many people in their effort to explain this gift have identified it as the "gift of discernment." However, there is no such thing mentioned in the Bible as a gift of discernment. Discernment is not a gift. Discernment is the natural act of exhibiting keen insight or good judgment. We could also describe discernment as being good old-fashioned common sense. For example, if you were to drive by your neighbor's house while they are away on vacation and you see someone unexpectedly inside with a mask on who is carrying a gun in one hand and jewelry in their other hand, you would quickly discern that this individual is a thief. You would immediately call the police and endeavor to see this person apprehended. Discernment is having the ability to know the difference between what is right and what is wrong.

When we are filled with God's Word, we will have the ability to discern between good and evil. We will only make good judgments when we weigh them in the light of the Word of God. When we make choices that reflect the opposite view of the Bible, then we lose our discernment and descend into a spiritual fog where there are no set boundaries for right or wrong. It's possible for a majority of people in a city, even a nation, to lose their discernment and make poor choices that are not in agreement with the expressed will of God. Always remember that God's Word is His will. It is not possible for the Word of God and the will of God to oppose each other. They will be in agreement at all times. God spoke to Jonah the prophet the following words:

> *And should I not pity Nineveh, that great city, in which are more than one hundred and twenty thousand persons who cannot discern between their right hand and their left—and much livestock?* (Jonah 4:11)

Here we see that God equates discernment with distinguishing the difference between what is morally right and morally wrong.

True discernment is based upon a system of beliefs that are grounded in God's Word. The citizens of Nineveh were spiritually bankrupt because they possessed no moral compass. God actually had pity on them because of their moral confusion. When you walk in the light of God's Word, your discernment between right and wrong will develop with laser-like precision. We all should have natural discernment, but discernment is not a spiritual gift.

Others have attempted to describe the gift of discerning of spirits as being some type of rare classification of elite Christians who have an unusual ability to discern the mysteries of God. They say that those who have this mysterious quality of spiritual discernment are able to properly interpret God's Word and are able to teach it correctly. They are rumored to be intellectual giants who are proficient in the Hebrew and Greek languages. But there is no such thing as a gift of spiritual discernment. The Holy Spirit will help all understand the Bible when they are willing to study it and prayerfully meditate about what they have read. While some Scriptures may initially be difficult to understand, they can eventually be comprehended through prayerful study. The Bible was never written by God to be understood by only a simple few who have some special quality of spiritual discernment.

The incorrect views concerning the biblical gift of discerning of spirits usually stem from not understanding that this is a supernatural gift. In other words, you can't place it in the category of the physical or mental realm. This gift should be elevated into its proper place of being supernatural, and thus operating through the Christian believer by the enabling power of the Holy Spirit. The nine gifts of the Holy Spirit are all supernatural in their function.

Discerning of spirits is not a "gift" of being suspicious. You don't need to be suspicious about people unless they give you reason to be. People who practice the sin of gossip often hide behind a pretense of being "discerning." They disguise their sin with a false humility, while they ask questions and endeavor to find out about things that are none of their business. They try to dig up people's past sins that have been washed away by the blood of Christ. They do not walk in a spirit of love; they suspect to discover some new "dirty laundry" that they can run and report to the religious authorities. If they don't find anything sensational to gossip about, then they create a story or exaggerate something out of context.

Once when Kelly and I were dating, in the days before we were married, we went out to dinner and had a nice meal and fellowship together. When we returned from dinner it was about 8 o'clock in the evening. Kelly dropped me off at the house where I was staying—a home that an elderly Christian single woman owned. She rented out rooms in her house, and I and five other Christian single men lived there, each in our separate room. Before I got out of the car, we talked a little bit. Naturally, Kelly turned off her car engine and we sat there and talked for about fifteen minutes. We were parked in front of the house beneath a street lamp and everything was well lit. When it came time to say goodbye, Kelly attempted to start her car, but it wouldn't start. For some reason the battery had gone bad. Kelly had her car insurance card in her purse with the phone number to a local tow truck company. Her insurance provided a free battery jump, so we called the company and waited for the truck to come.

The company said they would be there in an hour, but it ended up taking two hours for them to arrive. But as soon as they jumped the battery her car immediately started up and she drove home. The next day she had a new battery installed to resolve the problem. This happened on a Monday night. On Wednesday night we went to church for the mid-week service. Upon arriving in the church foyer, the assistant pastor met me and asked me to come into his office, along with another church elder. As I sat down, the assistant pastor said, "Steven, Sister E... (who was my landlord) came to the church yesterday and reported that she saw you and Kelly commit fornication on Monday night. She said that you both had "fallen in sin" and that she witnessed the act take place in a car in front of her house.

When he told me this I was shocked. With disbelief I said, "It's completely untrue. With God as my witness, I have never touched Kelly in an improper way." The assistant pastor and the elder looked at me with a grim face. Then, to my relief, they slowly smiled and began to gently laugh. The associate pastor said, "Steven, we were confident that this woman's accusations about you and Kelly were untrue. We do have to check all reports we receive. But the majority of everything this woman tells us is nothing but lies and slander. Here in the church offices we refer to her as our 'resident spirit of gossip.' Thanks for your time. You have nothing to fear. We will make sure that this false report never spreads."

While we do keep our guard up against the strategies of the devil, we do not, however, choose to view people with suspicion or a critical spirit. To be suspicious or to be critical is not a gift of the Holy Spirit. Let's now take a biblical look at what discerning of spirits is according to the Bible.

Discerning of spirits is a manifestation of the Holy Spirit that allows you to see, hear, taste, touch, or smell in the realm of the spirit. Most people possess five physical senses. These five senses are also present in the spirit realm, although in the spirit realm they can function on a much higher level.

Discerning of spirits includes the realm of evil spirits which would also consist of demons and even Satan himself. The spirit realm also involves holy angels, redeemed saints, and God. Human spirits must also be taken into account because their intents and actions can be discerned by the Holy Spirit. This is a marvelous gift that reveals keen insight to operations going on behind the scenes that our natural senses are not capable of knowing.

Of the different ways in which this gift can operate, the one which happens to me most often is through the spiritual sense of smell. Have you ever smelled in the realm of the spirit?

THE SPIRITUAL SENSE OF SMELL

Once I was attending a Christian conference overseas. I was one of the main conference speakers, and I knew all of the other speakers except one person who was not mentioned on the conference brochure. The speaking sessions were going exceptionally well until it came time for the minister to speak whom I had never met before. I decided to stay to watch her minister. My wife was sitting next to me when this person began to speak. As she began talking she shared what started off as a good message, but then she started drifting over into some strange things. At about this point the unmistakable smell of a skunk came wafting strongly into my nostrils. The smell was so thick that it seemed an actual skunk had walked into the meeting and sprayed the whole room with the foul odor. This was a supernatural smell.

Others in the meeting did not smell it. I smelled this in the spirit realm. After smelling this odor for about half a minute, my wife Kelly turned to me and said, "There's a skunk up there ministering. That woman is operating in occult power, and she stinks like a skunk." "Yes," I responded, "but there's nothing I can do because the conference host has given her permission to minister to the people."

We watched as this woman caused some major problems that disrupted the conference and sowed confusion among the people. God is not the author of confusion, but of peace. She was a false prophet who had evil spirits working through her to work false signs and wonders. The host for the conference was a very good minister, but he was deeply disturbed by what she did. Following this episode he broke ministry relationship with her and made a commitment to never invite her back. Even though this woman appeared to operate in supernatural power, she never deceived me or my wife for a moment. The Holy Spirit alerted us to her deceit by the smell of the skunk.

A long time ago I learned that just because something appears to be supernatural does not necessarily mean it is from God. I found out later that this woman had a long track record going back over two decades of faking miracles and deceiving people for personal financial gain. She had been reduced to traveling outside her home country and going places where she hoped no one would recognize her true identity. This is one example of how discerning of spirits can operate. As a child of God, the Holy Spirit loves you and He will endeavor to protect you from evil through these means of spiritual communication. Smell is a very clear-cut way of swiftly communicating a specific message.

At other times I often smell heavenly fragrances as I minister. Roses would be the foremost fragrance, followed by the smell of many different varieties of perfume. When the wonderful fragrances of heaven are being emitted, it means the anointing of God's Spirit is working in the lives of those present. Each smell has a particular meaning that God is trying to convey. Often when I smell or taste mint while ministering, it means that God desires me to begin praying for the sick. Over the years I have learned to identify mint with God's desire to heal. Whether the fragrance is good, bad, sweet, or something that smells awful, we need to seek the Lord for the meaning of what we are experiencing.

There is a certain fragrance that comes forth in my meetings when there is a high level of God's anointing present to work miracles. When I pray for a person and a creative miracle happens, I have discovered that this specific fragrance is always manifested. The smell is very thick and dense. It is not a sweet floral smell, but more on the low ends toward some type of musk. It is very pleasing to smell and it is definitely not from this world.

Once while I was in Israel, I was asked to pray for a teenage boy who had flat feet. His mother told me he was born with no arches in his feet. The boy was 14 years old. I asked him to sit down and take off his shoes and socks. At this time I had just finished praying for about 200 sick people. Most of the people had left except for a small group of about twenty people. I asked those remaining, "How many of you would like to see a miracle? Then come close and watch what God is going to do."

I held one of his feet in my hands, and I was going to pray for him using the authority of the name of Jesus. But before I could even pray a short prayer, I could feel the bones in his foot moving. Within three seconds a perfectly formed arch appeared in his foot. I took the other foot and held it in my hands, and it also had an arch appear in just a few seconds. The whole time this was taking place I could smell that specific heavenly fragrance that accompanies my ministry when a creative miracle occurs. It's like having wind blowing in your sails, a gentle push from heaven that lets you know that God is with you. The boy and his mother were deeply touched by God's love and power. Our small group all saw the creative miracle that God performed with our own eyes.

Throughout history, many men and women of God were aware of a specific fragrance that would be associated with their ministry. The Catholic priest from Italy, Padre Pio, was known for the sweet smell of violets that would emit from him. He never wore any cologne but the particular fragrance of violets always seemed to be coming off of him. Catholics speak of this as the "odor of sanctity." It refers to a fragrance proceeding from a person, their clothing, or their presence. It also is suggestive of a holy walk with God.

Saint Francis of Assisi is said to have smelled of lemon. Saint Rose smelled of rose (seems rather fitting), Saint Cajetan smelled of orange blossom, Saint Lydwyne's fragrance was a compilation of several aromas including cinnamon, ginger, clove, rose, and violet. It was said the breath of Blessed Herman of Steinfeld was like a garden full of beautiful flowers. Saint Catherine smelled of violets. Others were accompanied by fragrances that were so unworldly in their beauty that the specific smell could not be categorized with anything we are familiar with on earth.[1]

Sister Giovanna Maria of Roveredo, Italy, was a nun who committed her life to the Lord to live in celibacy. In a vision the Lord Jesus came to her and placed a wedding ring on her finger, indicating a spiritual espousal. From that time onward her finger emitted a beautiful fragrance which she could not hide. If someone touched her finger, the fragrance would be transmitted to that person for a few days. Eventually the perfume extended from her finger to her whole hand, then to her body, and then to every object she would touch. Those in her community said the fragrance was an indescribable sweetness. It would always be strongest upon her whenever she returned from Communion. The fragrance exuded from her, from her clothes, even from the straw mattress upon which she slept. If the other nuns wanted to find Giovanna, they would simply follow her fragrance to where she was. Her biographer pointed out that the intensity of this supernatural fragrance would increase or decrease according to the biblical calendar. On the Jewish feast days, the fragrance upon her would reach its climax; while on other normal days it would be more subdued.

Maria Angeli lived in Turin, Italy, and was born into a noble family. At the age of fifteen she became a Carmelite nun. Many attested to the sweet fragrance that followed her. It was also said that the heavenly fragrance would increase more strongly upon her during the days of the biblical feasts, particularly the Feast of Pentecost, Passover, and also during Christmas time. When Maria was promoted to the position of Mother in the convent, the other nuns would try to find her by first looking in her small cell, if she wasn't there they would track her by the fragrance she left. In her humility Maria tried different tactics to avoid being an object of attention, even going so far as carrying foul-smelling objects into her room, but it was all to no avail. The Lord chose to anoint her with His beauty and it could not be hidden.

Discerning of spirits is the ability to see, hear, taste, touch, or smell in the spirit realm, as the Holy Spirit allows. Whenever you smell a spiritual fragrance, it is because the gift of discerning of spirits is in operation. We have looked at how it is possible to smell in the spirit realm, but we must also consider the potential to *taste* in the spirit realm. We have the following Scriptures to validate such divinely granted experiences.

TASTING IN THE SPIRIT REALM

Oh, taste and see that the LORD is good (Psalm 34:8).

Now when I [Ezekiel] looked, there was a hand stretched out to me; and behold, a scroll of a book was in it. Then He spread it before me; and there was writing on the inside and on the outside, and written on it were lamentations and mourning and woe. Moreover He said to me, "Son of man, eat what you find; eat this scroll, and go, speak to the house of Israel." So I opened my mouth, and He caused me to eat that scroll. And He said to me, "Son of man, feed your belly, and fill your stomach with this scroll that I give you." So I ate, and it was in my mouth like honey in sweetness (Ezekiel 2:9-3:3).

Then the voice which I [John] heard from heaven spoke to me again and said, "Go, take the little book which is open in the hand of the angel who stands on the sea and on the earth." So I went to the angel and said to him, "Give me the little book." And he said to me, "Take and eat it; and it will make your stomach bitter, but it will be sweet as honey in your mouth." Then I took the little book out of the angel's hand and ate it, and it was as sweet as honey in my mouth. But when I had eaten it, my stomach became bitter (Revelation 10:8-10).

These Scriptures speak to us of the ability to eat and distinguish flavors in the spirit realm. Many of God's people have never experienced what it is like to taste in the spirit realm, but God wants us to taste and see that He is good; He wants us to know the reality of His goodness in a tangible way. In 2011 I was ministering in Taiwan when we had a strong manifestation of "tasting" in the spirit realm. Before ministering, I had the opportunity to spend the day in prayer and preparation for a late afternoon meeting. During this time of preparation the Lord impressed upon my heart the following Scripture:

I am the Lord your God, Who brought you out of the land of Egypt; open your mouth wide, and I will fill it (Psalm 81:10).

The Lord gave me a promise that He would fill the mouths of the people with a heavenly substance during my time of ministry. When it came time for me to speak, I taught for about one hour and then allowed the Holy Spirit an opportunity to minister to the audience. I instructed the people to worship the Lord; and as they worshiped, they had a heavenly substance placed in their mouths to eat. Within a few minutes hundreds of people experienced having heavenly food placed in their mouths.

It's always amazing because the Lord understands cultural differences, so the heavenly food corresponds to the local taste preferences of the people. The food that was first placed in the mouths of the people was Chinese eggrolls. This appeared to be the appetizer. Next up for the main course was an Asian version of a popular meal of meatballs and green beans. It didn't taste like American meatballs, but it had an Asian spice that all the people loved. After a big taste of eggrolls, meatballs and green beans, the Lord followed up with dessert by supernaturally putting chocolate in the mouths of the people!

It seemed that the women had a particularly strong experience of eating the chocolate. One Taiwanese woman who loved the culture of Europe had French macaroons put in her mouth. We had moved over into the glory realm and it seemed like anything was possible. The laughter, the uncontrollable joy, and especially the surprised looks on the faces of God's people were priceless.

After the experience of tasting in the spirit realm, I informed the people that they would now "smell" in the spirit realm. In my hand I was holding a twenty-ounce bottle of drinking water that I had not yet opened. Because of the strong manifestation that the Holy Spirit brought forth concerning tasting, my faith was high. Because the gift of special faith was on me, I felt like the Holy Spirit had given me a green light of divine permission to be creative in displaying the Lord's glory. What I did next was not specifically something the Lord directed me to do, but rather a choice to create something on the spot, and go with whatever my heart felt like doing. When the Lord is with you, He allows you to have freedom. He will back up your words because you are under His authority and care.

So, holding up the water bottle, I instructed the people, "Please sit down in orderly rows. I am going to open this water bottle and I will walk past you and sprinkle water on your eyes. Please have your eyes closed. When the water touches your eyes you will smell the fragrances of heaven." The ushers quickly went to work helping the people sit in neat, orderly rows. There were about 400 people present.

These were people from all walks of life who came from throughout Southeast Asia to the meetings deeply desiring to experience the glory of God. There were ministers, housewives, teachers, doctors, bankers, lawyers, businessmen and businesswomen—all taking a week off work to attend this conference in a remote mountain resort to meet God. The Lord will honor spiritual hunger. If you seek the Lord, you will certainly find Him.

Once they were seated, I opened the water bottle and walked past them with my wife walking with me. I used my fingers to liberally sprinkle the water upon the eyes of the people and the fragrance of roses burst forth in great beauty. Some people went into visions and saw scenes in heaven; others just laid back on the floor and breathed in the wonderful smell. It was as if countless bouquets of roses had been suddenly placed throughout the meeting room. Soon other fragrances began to materialize, with vanilla, orange blossom, and floral notes being clearly smelled.

These beautiful manifestations of the Holy Spirit draw people into a deeper walk with God. I have found over the years that when Jesus is exalted through the gifts of the Holy Spirit, it is very effective in empowering God's people to break free from the distractions of the world and thus pursue God with a clear and renewed focus.

Endeavor to be a multidimensional believer in which you are filled to overflowing with the Holy Spirit and are keenly aware of God's desire for you to operate in the spiritual gifts. Become comfortable with the gifts, anticipating that the Holy Spirit will minister through you with the gift that is most needed at that particular time. As you can see from our study in this chapter, the mysterious gift known as *discerning of spirits* can greatly assist you in your walk with the Lord. I pray that this beautiful gift will operate in your life from this day forward, and that your advancement in all nine gifts of the Holy Spirit will bring much glory and praise to God.

ENDNOTE

1. Valerie Ann Worwood, The Fragrant Heavens: The Spiritual Dimension of Fragrance and Aromatherapy (New York: Bantam Books, 1999), 84.

6

Super Faith—Nothing Is Impossible with God

But the manifestation of the Spirit is given to each one for the profit of all...to another faith by the same Spirit... (1 Corinthians 12:7,9).

In order to properly understand what the gift of faith is, we should have a basic understanding of how the Bible defines faith. There is a clear definition of the meaning of faith laid out for us in the following verse:

Now faith is the substance of things hoped for, the evidence of things not seen (Hebrews 11:1).

Faith is a belief, firm persuasion, or conviction that is based upon what you hear from the Bible. The word "substance" means a "firm substructure" like that of a poured concrete slab that would be used as the foundation for a new home. The word "evidence" means "proof" and it relates to proof of things we do not see with our natural eyes yet they are accepted based upon what God said. Faith works in conjunction with our hope. Hope is an expectancy that what God promised will come to pass in our lives. There are good things that we all hope for, and our faith is used to pull them into reality. To have faith is to take God at His word and believe Him. Your faith only feeds on one thing—the word of God.

> *So then faith comes by hearing, and hearing by the word of God* (Romans 10:17).

Faith does not come by hearing the news programs on television. Faith does not come by reading sports magazines or books about cooking. These things cannot feed your faith. If you will spend time daily hearing the word of God, then faith will come to you. When Paul the apostle ministered in Thessalonica, he persuaded a great multitude of Greeks to believe that Jesus is the Christ. However, many of the Jews were not persuaded and these unbelieving Jews gathered a mob and caused a citywide riot that threatened Paul's life. Paul leaves at night with his traveling companion, Silas, and they traveled to Berea. When they arrived, they went into the synagogue of the Jews. There was a noticeable spiritual difference between the Jews in Thessalonica and those in Berea.

> *These were more fair-minded than those in Thessalonica, in that they received the word with all readiness, and searched the Scriptures daily to find out whether these things were so* (Acts 17:11).

When you study the Word of God daily you become noble minded. The phrase "noble minded" actually means to "act with princely demeanor." It is enjoyable to read recreational magazines. But I don't know of any magazine that will cause you to start acting like a prince when you read it on a regular basis. The Jews in Berea did not just take Paul at his word because he was a good teacher. They checked up on his statements to see if they could be verified with the Scriptures. They took the time and effort to unroll the scrolls and search the Scriptures. The more time they spent studying what Paul had said, the more they were convinced from the Old Testament Scriptures that Jesus is the Christ.

Time spent in the Word of God produces eternal benefits, as we see in the next verse:

> *Therefore many of them believed, and also not a few of the Greeks, prominent women as well as men* (Acts 17:12).

All of the quality time they spent studying the Scriptures *caused them to believe* in Christ as their Savior. When they studied the Scriptures it did not produce doubt or fear. It produced faith—it always does. The gift of faith takes people beyond their normal ability to believe. It is best viewed as a special or extraordinary faith that comes upon you as the Holy Spirit desires. I refer to it as "super faith" because when it is in manifestation you feel tremendous boldness, and there is not a speck of doubt that can touch you while you are under the anointing of super faith.

This is not ordinary or common faith that we operate with on a day-to-day basis. For example, people can express faith that they believe the Bible is the inspired Word of God, composed of 66 books which reveal God's plan of redemption for humankind. People may also state that they believe that Jonah was truly swallowed by a large fish, just as it is recorded in the Bible. However, the *gift of faith* is different from the regular faith we possess that we use to trust in God's Word. Super faith comes by the Holy Spirit when we most need it. When this gift is in operation, our faith explodes to a phenomenal level. We have a supernatural ability to believe God for the impossible.

But Jesus looked at them and said to them, "With men this is impossible, but with God all things are possible" (Matthew 19:26).

When the gift of faith operates in you, it allows you to possess a portion of the same miracle faith that God has. It is a powerful gift that obliterates any surrounding atmosphere of doubt and unbelief. This gift empowers you to believe the impossible, and you do it with no strain, for this gift lifts you into a supernatural realm. This has nothing to do with will power or mental exertion. Keep in mind as we study each of the nine gifts that they are all supernatural. We are not referring to mental ability because faith does not originate in the mind but from within the heart of the child of God.

For assuredly, I say to you, whoever says to this mountain, 'Be removed and be cast into the sea,' and does not doubt in his heart, but believes that those things he says will be done, he will have whatever he says (Mark 11:23).

Jesus places an emphasis on keeping doubt out of your heart. This is not referring to the physical blood-pumping organ, but the spirit within a person. Sometimes doubt and an inability to see a way in which an impossible situation can be resolved will challenge the intellect. From a mental perspective, a situation may seem impossible and the mind can have a tendency to be unsure about these types of things. But faith will work in your heart even if there is some doubt going on in your head. It is critical, however, not to let doubt seep into your heart. So the gift of faith operates in your heart and produces tremendous faith that will go far beyond what a person's mind has the ability to grasp.

Whenever a person is raised from the dead, the gift of faith is in operation. Once I was in a meeting where an apostolic friend I know shared his story of raising a baby girl from the dead who had died while he was conducting ministry in the jungles of Guatemala. The baby was only 13 days old and was severely sick. The baby died early in the evening despite the efforts to save her life by an American doctor who had traveled with the minister on this missionary trip. The doctor declared the baby dead, but the minister took the lifeless body in his hands and said to the baby, "You will live and not die, and you will declare the works of the Lord." He began to quietly pray and continually speak words of life over the baby for next nine hours as he held the baby and carried her around.

This man of God prayed throughout the evening and into the night as he held the dead child in his arms. At about 3 o'clock in the morning the doctor encouraged the minister to stop and face the reality that the child was gone. But the gift of faith was working in this man and he knew he was soon going to see a miracle. At about 6 o'clock in the morning, after 12 hours of prayer and supernatural faith, the Lord did a miracle and sent the child's spirit back into its body. Today that baby girl is now a full-grown woman who is married, has three children of her own, and is faithfully serving the Lord. The Holy Spirit carried the minister beyond a place where his normal faith could reach and the gift of faith allowed him to believe for a miracle.

SUPER FAITH BOLDNESS

The gift of faith will produce tremendous boldness that surges through you like an electrical current. The Holy Spirit often moves upon me with this gift when I am ministering to people in prayer lines and conferences. But it also can potentially come upon you at any time of day or night if the Holy Spirit decides to manifest it.

For instance, in the summer of 1997 I was driving south down Harbor Boulevard in Orange County, California. It was 12 o'clock noon, and I was running a few errands. While driving, I was suddenly overcome with the most intense hunger for food. Although I had a large breakfast earlier in the morning, I could not resist the need to immediately eat. The intense hunger was so unusual that my mouth began salivating, and I felt like a person who just finished an extended fast—although I had not been fasting. I said to myself, *I've got to take the first exit and find the nearest fast-food restaurant because I feel like I'm starving.*

With great zeal I turned right at the next exit and at once saw a Jack in the Box hamburger restaurant. I parked my car and almost ran into the restaurant to order my food. Stepping up to the counter, I ordered a large drink, double cheeseburger, and a large French fries. After a few minutes my food was ready, and I took it in a to-go bag so I could sit in my car and eat it. With great anticipation I took the food out of the bag, removed the paper wrap off the cheeseburger, said a quick prayer of thanksgiving, and held the burger up to my mouth. The moment I did, the intense hunger that had been in me vanished. I was left thinking, *What am I going to do with all of this food?* Then I looked up and saw what I had not noticed before. At that moment the Holy Spirit came upon me with super faith.

Because of my unworldly appetite, I had rushed into the restaurant extremely fast without noticing a group of people standing outside the double-glass doors. Now that I was sitting in my car, I could see four people standing next to the entrance doors. There were two women and two men who all appeared to be in their early twenties. They each looked like they would comfortably fit in a street gang and they appeared to be in the mood to start trouble with the first person who would challenge them. Two stood on each side of the doors with their backs and one foot against the wall just waiting for a fight. They were heavily tattooed with gang symbols, wore dark headbands and appeared agitated and aggressive. One of the guys was particularly large and wore a tank top that revealed huge bulging muscles. His neck looked as big as a bull's, and he possessed a thick muscular chest like that of a male gorilla. His twenty-inch arms were enormous and they were rippled with definition. I could now understand why the restaurant was empty. Anyone driving into the parking lot would see this group of troublemakers blocking the way in, and would just turn around and go somewhere else to eat.

With super faith surging through my spirit, I grabbed my cheese-burger and got out of the car and walked toward them. I went right up next to the big-muscle guy and leaned my back against the wall and put one of my feet behind me up on the wall just as they were doing. I took a bite of my cheeseburger and smiled at them as they glared at me with detestable looks. Then the big guy turned and reached his big hands toward me. I knew exactly what he was going to do. I could see the devil in his eyes. He was reaching toward my neck to choke and strangle me.

But with tremendous authority I shouted, "In the name of Jesus!" When I did that, the Holy Spirit came mightily upon all four of them. Their legs buckled and they appeared to become like wax. Their facial expressions changed from intimidation and hate to instantly that of being terrified. They were bent over forward by an unseen force and were shaking before me.

The word of the Lord roared through me like that of a lion. With power I said, "Who do you four think you are to stand before these doors and intimidate and bully the customers of this restaurant? Have you no concern for the owner of this business who suffers financial loss at the hands of your foolishness? The Lord Jesus Christ calls upon each of you now to repent of your wicked ways, turn from your sins, and come back to Him!"

When I uttered these words, the four broke into deep weeping and sobbing. They became completely undone. At this point I thought it was best to walk them over to a place at the far edge of the parking lot so I could minister to them further. I instructed them to follow me and we soon reached a suitable place that was quiet. At this point they were still weeping uncontrollably and could barely stand up. Now that God had broken through to them, the Holy Spirit had me shift from a mode of divine power to that of soft and gentle compassion. I shared with them their need to make their hearts right with God.

With tears streaming down her face, one of the young women said with a trembling voice, "My daddy is a Pentecostal pastor. I have so dishonored God and my parents, God, please forgive me." One of the men then confessed while crying tears of grief, "My father also is a pastor of a Pentecostal church. God, please forgive me for having forsaken You." By the Lord's grace I was able to restore two of them back to the Lord and lead the other two into salvation in Christ! After praying over them, they no longer shed tears of sorrow. Now tears of thanksgiving for God's love and forgiveness ran down their cheeks.

Before they departed, I prayed a prayer of blessing over their lives. As they left I walked back to my car and sat down inside. I looked at the large order of fries, uneaten cheeseburger, and large drink. With a smile on my face, I slowly ate my food that had now gotten cold and thanked the Lord for the gift of super faith. I never did finish eating that large meal because I wasn't naturally hungry to begin with. But the meal and the salvation experience with those four young men and women certainly left a pleasant and satisfying taste in my mouth.

The unusual hunger that came upon me that day by the Holy Spirit was another spiritual gift in manifestation. We see in the life of Apostle Peter that he also had an experience of having a supernatural hunger come upon him.

> *The next day, as they went on their journey and drew near the city, Peter went up on the housetop to pray, about the sixth hour. Then he became very hungry and wanted*

to eat; but while they made ready, he fell into a trance (Acts 10:9-10).

I have discovered when a supernatural hunger (or thirst) comes upon me, it is the Holy Spirit preparing me for something that is about to happen. Peter was about to experience a powerful vision in which he was commanded by God in the vision to eat food that he did not want to eat. The words "very hungry" in the Greek language can be translated as "intense hunger." The Holy Spirit moved upon Peter while he was on the rooftop with intense hunger, and He moved upon me driving down the street in my car. This manifestation of the Holy Spirit is discerning of spirits, which we studied in the previous chapter.

When you move into a place of super faith, you feel very comfortable doing whatever it is that God is having you do. The gift of faith is really quite notable because it neutralizes doubt and fear, even if others around you are not backing you up with faith or prayers. For instance, when I pray for a sick person in front of several thousand people, I am trusting God to heal that sick person. This can feel extremely uncomfortable from a natural standpoint when it initially seems like nothing is happening.

Thousands are watching me, I feel the sweat roll down my back, and the devil makes mental suggestions such as, "It's not going to work here. You will be run out of town in shame and humiliation." I always pray for the sick even if there is no manifestation immediately of the healing gifts. But when the healing gifts are manifested, it is a world of difference that makes praying for the sick appear to be effortless. When the healing gifts and super faith are both in manifestation, I never feel awkward or intimidated by the sneers and unbelief of sinful humankind.

When super faith is in manifestation, it doesn't matter if you are surrounded by unbelievers, cynics, critical thinkers, or scoffers who are heavily present in the crowd. Their unbelief has no bearing on the results of your prayers. You are free to move in the Spirit unencumbered by the thoughts or aversions that others may have about you who do not understand the ways of God. This is why Jesus was so successful in ministering to people even when surrounded by the religious leaders who were constantly criticizing Him and hoping He would make a mistake. The gift of faith places a protective barrier around you and the unbelief of others simply does not affect you.

The gift of faith can come upon you when you have to speak to others about difficult matters. This gift can also be displayed through you during those times when you have to ask someone for something, such as asking for a raise or requesting a job transfer because of a family situation. Super faith can be there so that you ask in a confident way that then releases the favor of God that you need in order to get what you are asking for.

This gift can come upon you anywhere and anytime, so keep that fact in mind. If you ever find yourself in a place where your faith seems weak and you feel you can't go on, then the Holy Spirit will always be there to lift your faith to a supernatural level so that you are carried through to victory.

7

GIFTS OF HEALINGS—STILL THE DINNER BELL FOR THE LOST

But the manifestation of the Spirit is given to each one for the profit of all...to another gifts of healings by the same Spirit (1 Corinthians 12:7,9).

Concerning divine healing we have to ask ourselves a question and understand the scriptural answer in order to have the *gifts of healings* operate to their fullest potential. This question causes countless Christians to not receive God's healing power. The question is, "Is it God's will to heal?" In my teaching on this subject I have often shared that I have much higher results ministering God's healing power to unbelievers as compared to Christians who have been in the church for several years or longer. When unbelievers who are sick come to my meetings, they have often never been in a church service before. Most have never watched Christian television or had any direct exposure to the teaching of God's kingdom. In one sense it is easy to minister to unbelievers because they are like a clean chalkboard that has not been written on. I don't have to spend hours erasing wrong teaching from their minds because they have never had any religious teaching.

In such instances the healings with unbelievers are often instant and the success rate of them being healed is very high. I will first show them Scriptures that express the will of God concerning healing. This builds their faith to receive from God. Upon being healed many turn their hearts to the Lord and receive Him as their Savior. The faith to be healed comes the same way as receiving eternal salvation does—by hearing the Word of God.

Just the opposite often happens with Christians who have been in the church for several years. Once saved, a believer is soon influenced by church doctrine that is taught from the pulpit which may either be right or wrong based upon the minister's understanding of the Scriptures. The particular denomination or stream of Christianity that they are in may also distribute written material and media, which also expounds their view of certain biblical subjects such as healing. Over a period of time, a person forms a basis of beliefs from what is taught. Usually sheep eat whatever the shepherd (the pastor) feeds them. Outside of the Sunday morning service, some Christians will not open and study their Bibles until the next Sunday morning rolls around. So they simply believe what they are told. Very few search the Scriptures to see if what is taught is accurate.

While many teachings prove invaluable to the new believer, other teachings can be wrongly taught that hold back a believer from receiving all that Jesus purchased for them through His redemptive act at the cross of Calvary.

From childhood, my brothers and I were raised in church. We were there three times a week—every Sunday morning, Sunday night, and Wednesday night with our parents. I thank God that we were raised in church and had a basic understanding of the gospel message.

We were saved because we put our trust in Jesus and received Him into our hearts as Savior and Lord. But once we were saved and baptized in water, I never really progressed in my spiritual development because I was taught that once you were saved then everything was fine and one day you would go to heaven after you died.

This was difficult for me to comprehend because from a teenager's perspective, heaven was a long way off. I wasn't planning on dying anytime soon, so what was I supposed to do between being saved and eventually dying and going to heaven? It never occurred to me that I could have a walk with God that was exciting, adventurous, and full of experiencing the Holy Spirit's power.

Growing up in church, I had always been taught that God did not heal people in the modern-day age in which we now live. I was told that after the last apostle died in the days of the early church, the miracle power of God no longer operated. Various reasons were given in an effort to explain this view although they never really made sense to me. Finally I was told that I could not understand these concepts fully because I was not trained to read the Greek language of the original New Testament writings. As a young teenager I trusted what the church authorities taught me. I looked down on other believers from different denominations who did not hold the same views as my church did—for we were absolutely sure that we possessed all the truth and others who thought differently were deceived by the devil.

One fall at the beginning of the school year, my best friend was excited to see me and share with me about his summer experiences. We were best friends throughout high school although he was Pentecostal and I was on the opposite end of the Christian spectrum. He shared with me how he went to a summer Christian camp and was playing a game of baseball and seriously injured himself. While sliding into second base, he came in too fast and his left foot contacted the baseplate at an improper angle. He said he heard his ankle bone snap and he knew he had broken that bone. In extreme pain he lay there wondering what to do next. One of the men who was an assistant at the camp quickly arrived on the scene and with compassion and divine authority prayed for him, commanding the broken bone to be healed in the name of Jesus. Instantly he received strength in his ankle and then he stood up perfectly healed. My friend's eyes sparkled as he shared this story with me. He gave Jesus all the credit for healing him. He shared this openly with me while in sophomore English class.

Once he finished his story, I felt it was my duty to defend the beliefs of my church and hold high the banner of "No Modern-Day Miracles." With religious zeal I informed him there was no possible way for a broken bone to heal instantly. I suggested that surely he must have only slightly sprained his ankle and after having been prayed for, he experienced an emotional euphoria that overcame any temporary pain he may otherwise have experienced, thus allowing him to stand up pain free. Using arguments I had heard from the pulpit for why God can't perform miracles, I endeavored to strip away any hope he had of having received a genuine miracle from God. After a few minutes of my babbling rhetoric, he just looked at me and smiled and said, "Steven, you just don't get it, do you?" I laughed and said, "No, I would never believe anything as far out as what you have told me."

That day in English class I thought I had gotten in the last laugh on my friend concerning his summer healing experience, but God has a way of always ending up with the last laugh. After graduation it wasn't long before we lost track of each other as we branched off into different paths in life. Twenty years went by with no contact at all. But when the first forms of social networking emerged, it suddenly linked people together who had formerly lost touch. So, he got the last laugh when twenty years later he tracked me down and found my ministry Web site and saw that I was a Spirit-filled minister traveling the world and praying in the name of Jesus for the sick to be healed. He emailed me and rejoiced to see that I was preaching the full redemptive work of Christ.

FAITH COMES BY HEARING

So, you can see that I was a person whose chalkboard needed some things erased from it and the right information then written in. No matter who you are or where you live, the process works the same today as it always has in the kingdom of God. It's a very simple process, which is—faith comes by hearing. There's no need to reinvent the wheel because this method effectively works. You may be wondering how I went from a person who adamantly opposed divine healing to one who now ministers it to others on almost a daily basis. The change didn't happen overnight.

One summer while in college, I decided to take a temporary job that would last for two and a half months. It was a simple job although at times it was quite mundane. I was an apple tree pruner at a small apple orchard. There were 3,000 apple trees of different varieties, and each tree needed pruning so that it would later produce the most productive harvest. There was a work team that included me and five other college students. From 10 o'clock in the morning till 3 o'clock in the afternoon we would spread out and work on the trees. To help pass the time I had a small portable radio that picked up all the local stations in the area. There was a Christian station that I enjoyed because they played good Christian music. They also had certain preachers on the air that came on with prerecorded messages at varying times throughout the day. There was one preacher I greatly enjoyed listening to. Each day I looked forward to his program with great anticipation. He seemed to possess an authority in Christ that produced strong messages of faith and continual miracle healing testimonies. His name was R.W. Schambach. This dear man of God has now completed his earthly life and ministry. I look forward to meeting him one day in heaven where he now is.

Each day I listened intently to Brother Schambach's messages. He was a classic Pentecostal preacher with an emphasis on faith in God and strong demonstrations of the power of the Holy Spirit. His messages inspired me because of the hope they contained. They also fascinated me because of the constant mentioning of God's healing power. Slowly, over a period of weeks I began to entertain the thought that the messages he was preaching were in correct line with the Bible. My old theology was being pruned away just like the excessive apples on each tree that I carefully was removing.

After two months of listening to his daily program, I had erased twenty years of misinformed teaching that I formerly heard from the church pulpit when growing up that said, "God no longer does miracles today, and God no longer heals." In my free time I began to study the Bible like never before. My way of thinking and my way of speaking began to completely change. I felt like a young child in a candy store. While working at the apple orchard, I had been feeding my faith. It was like priming the pump to get it ready to start up. At the end of the summer, I was visiting a small Charismatic church when I was mightily filled with the Holy Spirit. Without the initial phase of hearing the Word of God preached through Brother Schambach for several months, I would not have had a scriptural foundation to receive the baptism in the Holy Spirit and the understanding that God is a healing God.

I would like to share with you my five favorite Scriptures that I believe are more than plentiful to convince any person with an open mind that it is the will of God to always heal. There are many other Scriptures that reveal God's plan to heal the bodies of sick people, but if a person will not receive five Scriptures than I have discovered they would not accept five hundred. So, let's briefly review these five

Scriptures and confirm from the Bible that it is the will of God for people to be healed.

FIRST SCRIPTURE

But, beloved, do not forget this one thing, that with the Lord one day is as a thousand years, and a thousand years as one day. The Lord is not slack concerning His promise, as some count slackness, but is longsuffering toward us, not willing that any should perish but that all should come to repentance (2 Peter 3:8-10).

Here we see that it is the expressed will of God that no one should perish and go to hell. Yet, every day there are those who die in their sins and enter into hell. Why do they perish in sin and go to hell? Because they did not accept Jesus as their Savior while alive upon the earth. Even though it was not God's will for them to perish, their rejection of Christ seals their eternal doom. With this reality in mind, I have often heard some people speak incorrectly concerning God's will to heal. I have heard countless believers say, "If it is God's will to heal me, then He will heal me when He is ready." To make a statement like this is to also say, "If it is God's will to save me, then He will save me when He is ready."

God is not going to save you, or heal you, unless you choose to receive it by faith. God doesn't overpower anyone and force them to be saved. God freely offers salvation, but unless a person receives it, that person will perish in his or her sins. God freely offers healing, but He absolutely will not force it upon anyone. If a person desires to receive healing, then that person must accept it by faith the same way one accepts salvation through faith. If you don't accept salvation, you miss out on heaven. If you don't accept healing, you miss out on being healed. It's really that simple.

Some believers have personally told me, "If it is the will of God for them to be healed, then God will just go ahead and heal them whenever He wants to." But that type of thinking does not line up with what the Bible teaches. For instance, do you think that God wants everyone to be saved? We know He wants all to be saved because God is "not willing that any should perish." Because God is so loving and kind, wouldn't you think that if there were any way possible for God to save everyone on planet Earth that He would do it right now? However, God cannot save everyone because not everyone wants to be saved. We are not created as robots to mindlessly follow orders. We have a will and the right to freely choose. To suggest that God will heal you if He just randomly feels like doing it, is to advocate that God will just randomly save some while others perish. God saves and heals through the same process of faith.

If God could heal everyone right now, He would. But He can't unless individuals choose to receive healing by faith. All of the promises of God must be received by faith. They don't just fall on you because you are a believer. All of the promises of God are "yes" and "amen," but you must possess the promises or else they will not do you any good. The promise of salvation is the greatest promise found in the Bible. But as beautiful as it is, it will be of no benefit if a person who is knowledgeable about it does not take it by faith. A sick person may be informed that it is God's will to heal him or her. The person may consider it to be wonderful news. But unless the person takes the promise of healing by faith, then it will have no effect in his or her life.

SECOND SCRIPTURE

When He had come down from the mountain, great multitudes followed Him. And behold, a leper came and worshiped Him, saying, "Lord, if You are willing, You can make me clean." Then Jesus put out His hand and touched him, saying, "I am willing; be cleansed." Immediately his leprosy was cleansed (Matthew 8:1-3).

The leper who approached Jesus and worshiped Him knew that if Jesus wanted to heal him then He certainly possessed the anointing to do so. What he had uncertainty about was whether or not Jesus was *willing* to heal him. It was not a question of ability; it was a question of the will of God. Jesus said, "I am willing." If Jesus would have responded in any other way, then we would all have reason to entertain doubt concerning the will of God to heal. If Jesus would have said, "No, maybe, or come back tomorrow," then we also would be justified for being uncertain of the will of God. But Jesus never once responded with uncertainty concerning God's will to heal. This Scripture alone should be enough to remove the "lottery mentality" that many believers hold.

A lottery mentality suggests that you never know for sure how God is going to react concerning healing. It implies that God randomly chooses to heal some while He decides to let others stay sick. Such believers view God as being in a constant change of mind. If God is in a good mood, He may reach His arm over the balcony of heaven and aim a healing laser gun down to the earth. Taking aim at a random individual Christian, He fires His gun and zaps the person with healing power. The person discovers that he or she is healed, but has no idea why God chose to bless. Such believers often make statements like, "God is very mysterious, you just never know what He is going to do." But that projected image of God is not the Jesus I see when I read through the four Gospels.

The devil operates on a system of random luck, chance, and lottery participation. When you look at how a casino operates, you have to understand that the majority of the odds are stacked in favor of the casino. A gambler may have a few wins here and there, but in the end the casino always wins because the whole method of operation is designed to take away a gambler's money. Jesus does not play the lottery, and He never operates from a lottery position. Healing is freely offered to all. He paid for it in full at Calvary. He does not choose who gets healed by having the angels roll dice and determine who gets a lucky day to be zapped with the healing laser gun.

Healing is not based upon getting lucky with God. If it were, then your outcome would be relegated to chance. What if your salvation was left to be decided in the same fate? Think about how cruel and unfair that would be. We should not view God as a lowly sinful human sitting in a smoke-filled room with a glass of whiskey in one hand and poker cards in the other hand. Albert Einstein expressed his own opinion concerning this as well: "God does not play dice."

If a believer views divine healing as being received solely upon the random discrepancy of God, then it is time to move from the lottery mentality over into a biblical mentality. Move from the devil's turf of illusion, uncertain results, and odds stacked always against you—and come into the blessed place of faith in God where everyone stands on a fair and level playing field. For one to receive God's healing power, there must be a firm confidence that it is the will of God to heal.

THIRD SCRIPTURE

If any of you lacks wisdom, let him ask of God, who gives to all liberally and without reproach, and it will be given to him. But let him ask in faith, with no doubting, for he who doubts is like a wave of the sea driven and tossed by the wind. For let not that man suppose that he will receive anything from the Lord; he is a double-minded man, unstable in all his ways (James 1:5-8).

Wisdom and healing are two promises of God that we can receive when we ask in faith. It is God's will for us to walk in wisdom. If it were not His will then He would not offer us the ability to receive wisdom. It is God's will to heal, but healing must be accepted by faith according to the same process in which one receives wisdom. Both promises are acquired through faith.

Regarding wisdom, the Bible says, "let him ask in faith, with no doubting." If a person has doubts when asking about whether or not God will supply them with wisdom, they will not receive anything from the Lord. Notice how the word "anything" is used in reference to other promises of God that are received through the same faith transaction. The word "anything" includes wisdom, but it would also certainly include healing as well.

If a person says, "I have asked God to heal me, but I'm not sure if He will do it or not," then I can already inform you according to the Bible what that person will receive—nothing. "For let not that man suppose that he will receive anything from the Lord." The issue of doubt must be removed in order to move forward and possess what God said freely belongs to us. God is not withholding wisdom from His people when they ask for it. Neither is He withholding His healing power.

At the cross of Calvary Jesus paid the price through His bodily sacrifice to redeem anyone who would receive Him from the perils of spiritual death, sickness, disease, and every other form of defeat and suffering. He paid this ransom price of our salvation with His own blood. Since the price has already been paid, why would He hold back that which He died to make freely available to us? It brings great joy to the heart of God when we accept by faith the wonderful provision He made for us at Calvary.

We can receive wisdom when we need it by simply asking in faith and not doubting that He will abundantly give it to us. We can also receive healing for our injured, diseased, or sick bodies by asking in faith and removing any and all doubt that would suggest it is not God's will to heal. Standing firm on the promises of God and holding on to them without wavering is the biblical method of receiving God's best for our lives. Doubt is a thief that robs a person of the promises of God. If doubt is allowed to come in to a person's heart then it can rob an individual or an entire church of what rightfully belongs to that person. Doubt will evaporate like a morning mist on a hot day when you feed upon God's Word.

SCRIPTURE FOUR

...There He made a statute and an ordinance for them, and there He tested them, and said, "If you diligently heed the voice of the Lord your God and do what is right in His sight, give ear to His commandments and keep all His statutes, I will put none of the diseases on you which I have brought on the Egyptians. For I am the Lord who heals you" (Exodus 15:25-26).

Here we see, in the original Hebrew language, that one of the compound names of God is revealed as Jehovah Rapha. This can be literally translated as "The Lord Who Heals." If people are unsure if it is the will of God for them to be healed, then it would be beneficial to discover the full meaning of God's multifaceted name.

I have kept the same legal name that my parents chose for me at my birth up until this time, and I don't have any plans on changing it. On March 22, 1967, I was born in Oak Ridge, Tennessee. My parents named me Steven West Brooks. This name is attached to my social security number and many other documents such as my driver's license and passport. You have most likely also kept your name unchanged as well. There can be certain exceptions to this. Often in

America a bride will take the last name of her husband upon getting married. This name change is registered in the court system once she is officially married.

The character and loving nature of God has never changed. He is still "The Lord God Your Healer." If there was ever a verse in the Bible that came along later declaring that God went down to the county courthouse in Jerusalem and legally changed His name, and He is no longer legally called Jehovah Rapha, then we would have reason to doubt His will to heal. But He has always been and always will be a healing God. God loves to heal. His name denotes His character. It is always His will to heal.

God is not a part-time God who heals. He is not Jehovah Rapha on only Tuesday and Friday and can therefore only heal on those specific days. The holy name of Jehovah Rapha reveals that He is willing to heal every day those who come to Him in faith.

SCRIPTURE FIVE

But the manifestation of the Spirit is given to each one for the profit of all: for to one is given the word of wisdom through the Spirit, to another the word of knowledge through the same Spirit, to another faith by the same Spirit, to another gifts of healings by the same Spirit (1 Corinthians 12:7-9).

If it were not God's will to heal, then why would the Holy Spirit manifest the gifts of healings? This gift is brought forth by the Holy Spirit to affect a healing and a cure in the body of an injured, diseased, or sick person. This is a heavenly gift that is different from simply praying in faith for a sick person to be healed. The gifts of healings come upon a believer to minister to the sick in the power of the Spirit with a divine grace gift. When this gift is in operation, it can often be tangible in such a way that it is felt or noticeably discerned by the person receiving God's healing power.

For instance, I was in Jerusalem in 2009 where I had ministered in a conference that just concluded the previous day. Now that the conference was over I found a little free time to relax and leave the hotel and find a place to get a good latte. Our hotel was within walking distance of the Jerusalem main central bus stop/shopping center, and I knew there were several good coffee shops there. Kelly and I walked the one mile to the bus stop and found a nice coffeehouse. Once there, I sat down at a table in the corner and waited as Kelly stood in line to order our coffee drinks. As she was waiting in line and slowly moving forward toward the counter to place her order, she was surprised that two ladies in their mid-sixties suddenly cut in line in front of her.

Kelly didn't say anything because she sensed they were confused as to where the line originated, and she also felt compassion for them. As Kelly stood in line she heard the two ladies carrying on a conversation. They were discussing how much pain they were in because of their sick conditions. Kelly leaped into the conversation and said, "Are you ladies in pain?" One responded, "Yes, the pain in my back is killing me." The other lady said, "We are both suffering in severe pain." My wife then pointed to me sitting alone at the table and said, "That man is my husband, and he has an international healing ministry. If you go ask him, he will be sure to pray for you."

While sitting at the table, I could see these two ladies hobbling toward me with their cups of hot coffee in their hands. The pain in their bodies was apparent from the way they walked and also from the strained and grimaced looks on their faces. They sat down at the table and asked me if I would pray for them. To be honest, we all feel like we have those times when we just want to be alone. I had just concluded a four-day conference where I had ministered and prayed for many people. This exertion had left me feeling physically tired, plus I had operated on very little sleep during the conference. When these ladies asked for prayer, I could hear and feel their suffering through their voices. On the inside I had to reach down deep to stir up the anointing and trust the Lord for the Holy Spirit to flow through me.

As I sat there I looked at them each squarely in the eyes and with conviction said, "I will pray for you, but in order for this to work I have to pray using the authority of the name of Jesus." When I said that, one of the ladies became startled and said, "Shhhh! Don't say that name in here, you are liable to start a riot!" "Well," I replied, "I have to use His name because He is the one who is the Healer." "All right," they said with reluctance. "You can use that name but we refuse to have anything to do with that man named Jesus. We don't believe in Him and we want nothing to do with Him." They spoke the Lord's name with great disdain, but I knew in my heart they did it out of ignorance and they had also never seen an expression of God's love toward them. I briefly explained to them that I would lay my hands upon them and God's healing power would then flow into their bodies.

Looking at the first woman, I said, "Give me your hand." As I held her hand, a warm and tangible healing anointing began to flow out of my left hand and into her body. She didn't say anything, but I could tell she was receiving really well. Her faith was definitely connecting with God's healing power. I rebuked the pain in her body and commanded it to leave. I was endeavoring to do this as quietly as possible so that we wouldn't draw unnecessary attention to our table.

Then I looked at the other woman sitting at the table and I said, "You're next." When I stretched out my hand toward her, the Holy Spirit all of a sudden came upon me with great healing power. From my elbow down to my fingers, my left arm suddenly burst into a flame of spiritual fire! No one could see it as a physical fire, but I could feel the flames leaping off my arm like glorious waves of fire with tremendous heat. The lady jumped back in her chair with a shocked look and exclaimed, "My God! What is that?" Remaining calm in an effort to not disturb the other people in the restaurant, I said, "It is the healing power of God manifested as fire. When I touch you with my hand, the fire of God will consume your sicknesses and the symptoms of pain will leave your body." Reaching over I touched her with my hand and I said, "Receive, in the name of Jesus," and the fire of God was then transmitted into her body.

The other woman I first prayed for said, "When you laid your hand on me I began to feel like I was on fire. I thought they must have spiked my coffee…I'm burning up as I sit here!" We sat together for another few minutes as I briefly shared the love of Jesus with them. One lady looked at her watch and abruptly realized they had lost track of time. Their bus, which they were waiting on, was now at the terminal. They rushed to gather their belongings and quickly thanked me for praying for them. As they hurried off to catch their bus, I couldn't help but laugh softly as I watched them stagger back and forth while walking as they appeared to be somewhat intoxicated. The Holy Spirit was greatly ministering the love of God to these two Jewish ladies. I don't know the outcome of their spiritual situation, but I am thankful to have been able to sow seeds of divine healing in the name of Jesus that I believe will eventually lead to the salvation of their souls.

MIX FAITH WITH PRAYER

The gifts of healings must be administered to others in a spirit of faith. If you pray for people expecting nothing to happen, then you will receive exactly what you expect—nothing. Always mix faith with your prayers. Even when the Holy Spirit is manifesting through you with a spiritual gift, you must still use your faith to go along with that corresponding gift.

Two months ago on a Sunday morning, I prayed for a young boy of the age of five. His mother reported he had been severely grinding his teeth in his sleep all night long for the past three years. In faith I prayed for the young boy, and I rebuked an evil spirit that was tormenting him. I then released God's healing power into his body through the laying on of my hands. Later that night his mother slept next to him and she stayed awake all night long listening for any grinding, but he did not grind his teeth a single time, nor has he ever ground his teeth since. We see these and many other types of healings take place consistently. When you pray for the sick, you must always keep your eyes on Jesus and visualize the Lord healing the people.

If the nine spiritual gifts could be considered "fun," then I would have to think that the gifts of healings is the most fun gift because it makes me so happy when others are healed. Since there are so many sick and diseased people in the church and in the world, this gift will always be in high demand and in frequent use. Sometimes the healings are instantaneous, other times it takes a little while for the healing to fully come forth. But what joy it brings when someone has received deliverance from the devil's torment and affliction. It's fun to pray for the sick, especially when the healing gifts are in manifestation.

You will always have good results when you pray for people in faith and refuse to be moved by external circumstances. I have prayed for people when the gifts of healings were flowing through me. Often I have prayed for people in severe pain. I would lay my hands on them and pray for them while releasing God's healing anointing in their body. Some would leave the prayer line in just as much pain as when they arrived. But I do not let that throw me in any way, because many of these same people would call or email me and say that the following morning when they awoke, the symptoms had completely left their bodies. Always stay in faith and do not doubt that it is God's will to heal—and for His people to enjoy divine health.

8

Working of Miracles—
An Explosion of Power

But the manifestation of the Spirit is given to
each one for the profit of all...to another the
working of miracles... (1 Corinthians 12:7,10).

It's important to understand that the gift of *working of miracles* is different from the gifts of healings, which we have previously studied. A healing is a work that God does in your body to bring it back into health. But a miracle is different. A miracle takes you over into the creative power of God. These two gifts are as distinctly different from each other as a wrench is from a screwdriver. They each have a unique purpose, and one will not accomplish what the other can. Understanding the differences can prove very effective in how we minister to people.

Back in the early 1900s and up through the 1940s, the primary gifts that were exercised in the church were tongues and interpretation of tongues. In the 1950s, the Healing Revival broke out and lasted for about a decade. This move of God brought divine healing more into the mainstream culture of America. The giant tent meetings held by Oral Roberts, Jack Coe, A.A. Allen, William Branham, and other ministers were often packed to their fullest capacities. The healing ministers had the largest tents in the world at that time, with some seating over 20,000 people.

The 1960s and 1970s saw the Charismatic Revival, the Jesus Movement, and the Teaching Movement come forth that swept millions of souls into God's kingdom. The 1980s saw televangelism come forth and this has resulted in television programs now presenting the gospel 24 hours a day around the world. Because most Christian television networks are charismatic in nature, this has resulted in bringing to the body of Christ around the world an opportunity to see most of the gifts of the Spirit in operation. In the 1990s, we saw the ministry office of the prophet restored more fully back to the church. During this same decade the gift of prophecy and the word of knowledge began to be released on a much broader scale within the church. In the first decade of the 2000s, we saw the apostolic ministry restored and with it the promise of greater manifestations of the Spirit through the power gifts. As the body of Christ continues to come into maturity, we will see that the gifts of the Spirit will also increase in their intensity.

The gift of working of miracles is certainly not at this point a common occurrence in much of the church on the earth today. While it does occur consistently in "hot spots" around the world where outpourings of God's Spirit are under way, it is still for many believers a rarity to behold. However, we are living in the season where this gift will now become much more established in the church. Out of all the nine gifts, this particular gift has the ability to win multitudes to the Lord with one single stroke.

Recently the Lord told me that the church needs to stop viewing miracles in the same way as people perceive supposed sightings of Bigfoot. Many Christians say they believe in miracles but at the same time they confess they have not seen the type of miracles that offer overwhelming, convincing proof that would satisfy the non-Christians of their authenticity. It's similar to Bigfoot. Some people believe he is out there hiding in the deep forest of northwest America, but he never comes out so that we can get a good look at him. Any photos of Bigfoot sightings are always captured with a grainy image that is somewhat out of focus, thus lacking clear detail. Footprints of Bigfoot have been faked so many times that those who claim to have found his tracks can't be fully believed.

A healing service can take place and a woman is genuinely healed by the power of God and gets out of her wheelchair and walks. Yet some will say she was never sick, but only had mental allusions of being sick. When the minister spoke, he made her feel hopeful and this triggered endorphins to be released in her brain thus causing her to overcome her mental paralysis and she then got up out of the wheelchair. The skeptics say it was only a mental issue. But real miracles can leave even the harshest critics without a logical explanation for what they witnessed.

> *And seeing the man who had been healed standing with them, they could say nothing against it. But when they had commanded them to go aside out of the council, they conferred among themselves, saying, "What shall we do to these men? For, indeed, that a notable miracle has been done through them is evident to all who dwell in Jerusalem, and we cannot deny it. But so that it spreads no further among the people, let us severely threaten them…"*
> (Acts 4:14-17).

The Jewish leaders could not deny that a miracle had taken place. A man over forty years of age who was crippled from birth received a miracle of healing. It was undeniable even to the opponents of the gospel. Miracles offer a convincing proof that God is alive and working in the lives of men and women. Whether or not a person responds to the Lord with an open heart is each person's own choice. Some choose to believe and receive the Lord into their heart. Others, like many of the Jewish religious leaders, choose to harden their hearts even after witnessing a true miracle with their own eyes. Either way, genuine miracles have a way of drawing a line in the sand and give people of faith a valid reason to boldly move forward with God.

SUPER POWER

The working of miracles is one of the three power gifts, along with super faith and gifts of healings. I believe within the heart of every person God has placed a desire to be able to somehow make contact with His miracle-working power. Even unbelievers reach out through certain means in an effort to relate to a power that is beyond their own human ability. When I was young, I took an interest in comic books. I read most of the popular ones such as Spiderman, Superman, Batman, Captain America, Fantastic Four, and the Incredible Hulk. The lesser known super heroes were also fun to read, such as The Flash, Green Lantern, and Thor. Back in the mid-1970s no one who read comics probably had any idea that 35 years later all of these comic characters would become major motion pictures that would generate billions of dollars in the movie industry.

Why do young people (and quite a few adults) read comic books? Why do millions of people go see a movie about a fictional character who appears to lead a normal everyday life but who also possesses a secret power that he conceals that allows him to do super human feats? The reason we are drawn to these movies and their super hero characters is because God has placed within the heart of every person a divine hunger to experience the ability for good to overcome evil in a personal way that is often demonstrated through super-human strength.

When I was in my mid-twenties, I was at the church one day for several hours to do some basic cleaning. It was a relaxing Monday morning and the only two people at the church were the pastor and me. Several times a week I would volunteer to help out in this way. That day I decided to thoroughly vacuum all the carpet in the sanctuary. Along the way I would stop and clean all the pews, picking up any gum wrappers or loose pieces of paper or trash. Starting at the front of the church, I worked my way back row by row until I reached the last and final row of the sanctuary. Sitting on the end pew were three comic books that appeared to be new that someone had brought to the church and had forgotten to take home.

Glancing at them I noticed they were three special edition Superman comic books. I gathered them up and marched them back to the pastor's office to report that an unknown person had been behaving in a sacrilegious way by bringing comic books into the holy sanctuary. Although I had been filled with the Holy Spirit for several years, I still hadn't yet been completely delivered from all of my former religious ways of thinking. With religious pride, I showed my pastor the comic books and told him that someone must had been reading them while he was preaching his sermon. My pastor was a godly man and could preach messages on holiness that would make you squirm in your seat. With a look that voiced deep concern my pastor took the comic books from my hand and with piety said, "Don't worry Brother Brooks, I will be sure to look into this and take care of it."

Having felt I performed my duty of defending the honor of God's house from material unsuitable for a holy religious establishment, I returned to my work of vacuuming and cleaning the church. After about fifteen minutes, I realized that I needed to tell the pastor that the vacuum cleaner needed new bags and that one of the deacons should pick some up at the store. As I walked back to his office, I noticed his door was open, so I just walked right in and caught him off guard. There he was leaning back in his big leather chair with his feet propped up on his mahogany desk with one of the Superman comic books open in his hands as he read it with rapt attention. With a startled look I exclaimed, "Pastor!" He looked at me with great surprise knowing that he was caught off guard and in a bind between religious expectations created by the whims of man and of one's own human nature that gravitates toward recreation that stirs your God-given imagination and desire to connect with a power beyond our own limited ability.

Sitting the comic book down on the table, he slowly broke into a deep laugh that bellowed up out of his spirit. He said, "Oh, Brother Brooks, the truth is that inwardly we all wish we could be super human in some way and be able to do things of an extraordinary nature!" His genuine laughter actually made me start laughing as well and I responded, "Yes, honestly I wish I could leap over tall buildings, fly, and shoot laser beams out of my eyes." We both laughed together and identified with a God-given attraction that we have in super power. The Holy Spirit brings forth the gift of working of miracles, which is a connecting bridge between humankind and the dynamic miracle power of God—allowing the two to come together.

SUPER HERO COMMITMENT

The gift of working of miracles was evident in the life of many biblical characters. Moses, Elijah, and Elisha had this gift operate often in their lives. Yet out of these men and many others in the Bible we see that one individual in the Old Testament possessed this gift in an unusual degree, making him appear to be a real-life super hero with a type of power that seemed to come from another world. Samson was a man who possessed a tremendous gifting but was not developed in character that could sustain the gift for a lifetime of effective service.

Just as Superman had a vulnerability to Kryptonite, so did Samson have an inherent weakness that eventually caused his downfall. Samson had some major character deficiencies that he refused to deal with and it ended up proving fatal for him. Always remember that your security is in your purity. If you compromise your purity, you will surely find yourself in the lap of some type of Delilah, getting a spiritual haircut and losing the anointing of God's Spirit. Samson was careless with the extraordinary gift that God had given to him. You must protect the anointing and value the grace to flow in the gifts.

The working of miracles is a very special gift and very few people have been blessed by the Lord to operate in this type of power. Many healing miracles that take place in the bodies of people have in the past been primarily inward miracles. But now is the time for inward and external miracles to come forth so that the Lord may be glorified. When you operate in working of miracles, you actually taste the power of the age to come. The kingdoms of this world will soon become the kingdoms of our Lord and of His Christ. The power gifts bear witness of the Lord's supremacy and His soon coming return.

Over the years I have noticed that any servant of God who operates in the working of miracles and sustains that gifting so that it operates consistently, is a person who is deeply dedicated to the truth of God's Word and will take those truths to heart and refuse to be swayed from them. Most believers that have this gift also spend quality time in prayer and usually also practice the spiritual discipline of fasting. Samson knew what it meant to live a fasted lifestyle because he was a Nazarite from birth. If you want to walk in miracle-working power, then the secrets of how to move into that gifting are found in the life and calling of Samson.

As a Nazarite he was required by God to abstain from certain pleasurable things that the other Israelites could enjoy. A Nazarite was required to abstain from drinking grape juice, wine, any fermented liquor and vinegar, or eating grapes or raisins. Abstaining from any product of the grape vine excluded a Nazarite from the normal social activities of regular people. A Nazarite was not allowed to come into contact with a dead body, even if it was a parent, brother or sister, or a treasured pet animal. Being separated from the corruption of death was a way in which a Nazarite would identify with his or her holiness through being linked with God's incorruptibility. When a person made a Nazarite vow to the Lord, it was either for a specified period of time or in some cases, like Samson, it was a lifetime commitment. During the entire period in which the vow lasted, the person was not allowed to cut his hair. The hair represented the core commitment of the Nazarite vow.

Samson flirted with sin too many times. He retrieved honey from the carcass of a dead lion. He threw a party for his friends which was primarily a drinking party. Scripture does not tell us if he drank wine but a dedicated Nazarite would get as far away from anything to do with drinking wine as possible in order to not be tempted. Despite these close calls, he did not have any catastrophic meltdowns until he divulged the secret of his strength—his hair. Immediately thereafter, his hair was shaved off through the deceptive tactics of Delilah.

When the gift of working of miracles flowed through Samson, he was invincible. There was nothing that the devil could throw at him to take him down when Samson was under the anointing. With his bare hands he tore a lion apart as easy as one would tear a piece of paper in half. He killed thirty men in Ashkelon. He caught three hundred foxes and tied them tail to tail, placed a lit torch in the middle, and released them to burn up the ripe harvest fields of the Philistines. He would snap thick ropes apart with ease, break bowstrings as easy as snapping a pretzel, and killed one thousand men in one battle with the jawbone of a donkey. Personally, I don't think Samson was this big and huge muscular man who exuded physical domination through a hulking physique. Why else would Delilah ask the question, "Please tell me where your great strength lies?" I believe he was a regular guy who possessed an extraordinary gift from God.

To operate in the gift of working of miracles, your life must be similar to the same principles that governed the life of a Nazarite. You must be consecrated to God, knowing that your life belongs to the Lord and your will must be submitted to His plan for your life. You must be dedicated to live a life of walking in the Spirit and not fulfilling the lusts of the flesh. And you must be content in knowing that because of your commitment (Nazarite vow), you will not always fit in or be in the limelight of the world's popularity. To operate in the gift of working of miracles requires a believer who is strong in faith and will be vigilant to maintain the Lord's wonderful presence in his or her life.

We live in a day where nothing can be hidden under a bushel. Almost all cell phones today have cameras. People are able to take images and videos with different devices and send them across the country and around the world within a few moment's time. All it takes to release a move of God's Spirit is to capture a mighty miracle on video, upload it to the Internet, then have it go viral by being pushed by social media sites. Within a few days, millions of people could see major miracles replayed before their own eyes on the Internet. What if someone had a smartphone and videoed Samson killing a thousand men with the jawbone of a donkey? What if they uploaded it to YouTube? Of course, those possibilities did not exist back then, but they certainly do today. Now it is possible for these great miracles to be seen by multitudes of people. The Lord knows what He is doing. The release of high definition technology has a kingdom purpose for displaying God's glory in the best quality possible. This is all part of God's plan to bring in the end-time harvest of souls.

You are not going to win many Hindus to Christ without miracles. You will not win to Christ many radical Muslims who have been taught principles of jihad from early childhood without them seeing convincing, miraculous proofs that verify Jesus is Lord. It is difficult for Buddhists to come to Christ without the miracle power of the resurrected Christ being presented before them. It's almost impossible to lead an atheistic or agnostic Jew to salvation in Christ merely through an oral presentation of the gospel. For thousands of years they have seen their prophets work mighty miracles. The Jews are used to miracles. This is characteristic of the Jewish people, and God is well able to oblige them by supplying their request in an effort to win them.

> *For Jews request a sign* [a miraculous proof, a divine distinguishing mark]... (1 Corinthians 1:22).

The working of miracles is an essential gift that God wants to utilize through His people in the conversion of lost souls to Christ. If the Lord is placing this mighty gift on your heart, seek Him for it and dare to believe that God can work miracles through you!

9

PROPHECY—STARGAZING WITH GOD

But the manifestation of the Spirit is given to each one for the profit of all...to another prophecy... (1 Corinthians 12:7,10).

Years back I was very excited one day because I had received new binoculars for my birthday gift. These weren't just an average set of binoculars, they were designed for long-range viewing of astronomical objects. They were so big and heavy that they had to be supported by a tripod in order for them to be properly focused. I had always wanted a pair of giant binoculars. And now I had these binoculars that possessed the ability to easily see the numbers and letters on a vehicle's license plate from over a mile away in distance. For several years I owned a "normal" pair of binoculars that proved useful for those random moments when I wanted to get a better look at something of interest that was beyond normal visual range. Wanting to progress further with my ability to clearly see things from a distance, I found an increased joy in stepping up to a more powerful model. With a smile on my face I took my new binoculars out for their first try.

In the back of my home was a large canyon that ran for a mile in each direction. Within the canyon were lots of rabbits and rodents that birds of prey loved to hunt. Suddenly in the sky I could see the form of a beautiful falcon descend and land in a cedar tree at the far northern edge of the canyon wall. I knew the falcon must have come to hunt for food and it might be possible to see him catch a snake or a lizard. This was my opportunity to view the world's fastest creature, the Peregrine Falcon. It can reach speeds in excess of 200 miles per hour when it dives out of the sky toward its prey. Quickly setting up my tripod, I placed my super jumbo-size binoculars on the stand and slowly focused in on the majestic bird who was a little over one mile away.

As the lens focus became perfect, I was stunned to see his short yellowish legs with his sharp brown talons wrapped firmly around the branch of the tree. Slowly I raised the binoculars and his chest and wings came into view. Without any strain I could see the striations in his grayish-white feathers. These binoculars were performing better than I expected. My heart was beating strong within me from the excitement of seeing something as beautiful as this amazing creature. I made one more quick adjustment by raising the lens angle to observe the bird's face. Upon leveling the binoculars with a straight on view of his head, I almost couldn't believe what I saw next. Looking through my binoculars, I saw that the falcon was looking directly at me with a riveting stare. It appeared he had been watching in amusement everything I had been doing. In fact, he seemed to be looking directly through the lens and was staring at me eyeball to eyeball. He had the funniest look on his face. In my best effort to adequately describe his facial expression, it looked to me like a whimsical smirk that was meant to say, "Nice try human, but I'm way beyond you when it comes to the ability of sight."

This experience left a humbling impression on me—that it is always of great value for us to seek God for a higher and longer range perspective on how He sees things. God can see into the future. He knows the beginning and the ending already. The gift of prophecy takes you beyond your own natural vision. It reaches beyond the falcon's great sight, and even our most powerful telescopes pale in comparison to the infinite vision of God. Prophecy releases your true potential and calling. It allows you to see what lies ahead of you and provides divine inspiration for you to attain God's purpose for your life.

Every time I used those binoculars I couldn't help but think of how awesome God's creation is. Often very late at night I would take those binoculars out during the cold winter months so I could view the moon, planets, and stars. The galaxies and nebulae were spectacular to observe. God's glory is revealed in the heavens. Because the universe in which we live is so awesome, I think that God has placed some element of a stargazer in all of us. Sometimes God uses object lessons when he prophetically speaks to us. When He wanted to demonstrate to Abram the vast offspring that would descend from him, the Lord took him outside and said:

> *"Look now toward heaven, and count the stars if you are able to number them." And He said to him, "So shall your descendants be." And he believed in the Lord, and He accounted it to Him for righteousness"* (Genesis 15:5-6).

Sometimes when we receive a prophetic word we feel as if we are in over our heads. We think, *How can this ever be accomplished? This is far beyond my ability to perform.* The true prophetic destiny we receive from God is always out of our natural reach. But with God's help nothing is out of reach. When Abram looked up at night and beheld the countless numbers of stars, he must have had a temptation to doubt what God said. How could he ever have as many descendants as the stars? Abram and his wife Sarai were well advanced in age and they still had no children. He must have been stunned by the prophecy that God personally spoke to him. But to his credit, we see that Abram believed what God told him and thus God accounted it to him as righteousness.

When Abram viewed the stars, he also caught a glimpse of the power of God. It dawned more deeply upon him that the Creator, who spoke all of those stars into existence and made the cosmos work in harmony, had infinite power that was beyond human understanding. The more you meditate on the complexity and size of the universe, the more humbled you are that such an awesome Creator with such mind-blowing capability would want to be your personal friend. The awe of it leaves you somewhat speechless. In response, Abram believed God, and then God made a special note of his act of faith and it was from then on considered a done deal before it ever happened. When Abram believed the prophecy it was accounted by God as an act of righteousness.

Many people do not realize that God is an accountant. In the eyes of God, accounting doesn't just involve numbers; God is looking for our faith, which He can accept and use as a deposit toward the manifestation of the prophetic word. Many prophecies are conditional and without faith they can't be fulfilled.

> And not being weak in faith, he did not consider his own body, already dead (since he was about a hundred years old), and the deadness of Sarah's womb. He did not waver at the promise of God through unbelief, but was strengthened in faith, giving glory to God, and being fully convinced that what He had promised He was also able

to perform. And therefore "it was accounted to him for righteousness" (Romans 4:19-22).

When a person initially receives a prophecy, they usually are excited. They may even write it down and keep it with them for a few weeks as a reminder. But when the prophecy doesn't come to pass within a few months or perhaps a year, then many forget and move on to a different focus. Delay can cause people to lose faith in what God said would happen. When faith begins to decline, then it may be even possible for a Christian to move into a mindset where prophecy is despised. Don't let your prophecies sit on a shelf and collect dust. Put them back before your eyes again and renew your faith in what God initially told you.

When a prophecy is spoken to you, it allows you to understand your God-given destiny in the same way that Abram understood his when he looked at the stars. God took Abram outside his tent on a dark and cloudless night with no light pollution and told him to look at the luminous stars. He may speak differently to you by informing you to go to the ocean, or sit by an airport, or climb up a tall mountain, or hike into a lush forest. God knows how to arrest your attention and speak to you through word pictures that are so clear they need no further explanation.

True prophecy unlocks your destiny. When you know your destiny you begin to dream of its fulfillment. When you begin to dream, you make plans to move toward the passion that is in your heart. Step by step as you walk with God, you go in the direction of your life's calling.

The devil has always tried to water down the gift of prophecy. The enemy wants us to lose our focus and forget what the Lord said to us. The way we overcome this is to honor the gift of prophecy and to also honor God's prophets.

Do not despise prophecies (1 Thessalonians 5:20).

This charge I commit to you, son Timothy, according to the prophecies previously made concerning you, that by them you may wage the good warfare, having faith and a good conscience, which some having rejected, concerning the faith have suffered shipwreck (1 Timothy 1:18-19).

When you receive a prophetic word from a prophet who is speaking under the anointing of the Holy Spirit, you are receiving a priceless gift that can be used as a catalyst for your faith. The devil will endeavor to bring into your life discouragement and negative circumstances in an attempt to foster doubt within your heart. The warfare in which you are engaged is a battle to stay in faith and hold on to what God promised you. Paul was reminding young Timothy of former prophecies he had received. Doubtless some of these prophecies were from Apostle Paul himself. Paul placed an emphasis upon believing true prophecy. There have been prophecies spoken to me in meetings by prophets who did not personally know me. But their prophecies confirmed the deepest and most treasured hopes within my heart. When we receive such strong and confirming prophecies, we need to let them inspire us to press on to their realization.

Pursue love, and desire spiritual gifts, but especially that you may prophesy (1 Corinthians 14:1).

We are told to desire spiritual gifts. The word "desire" in the original Greek language means to "burn with zeal, to be heated or to boil." According to this Scripture it appears that it is not enough to simply be open to the spiritual gifts. Some people say, "Well, if it's God's will for me to have a spiritual gift, then I am open to receiving it." Being open to receive is not the same as being on fire with burning passion to obtain the gifts. It is good to examine our hearts and ask the question, "Do I possess a burning passion that boils within me to operate in the gifts of the Spirit?" This is an apostolic mandate from

Apostle Paul, not an optional suggestion. Paul was trying to get the church to move into the greater gifts and not place an overwhelming emphasis on tongues. In the fourteenth chapter of First Corinthians he attempts to encourage them to desire prophecy in their corporate gatherings. The problem in Corinth was that those in the church were endeavoring to make their use of speaking in tongues a mark of their spirituality. Today many in the church have endeavored to use prophecy as an indicator of their spirituality and this can often confuse believers who are young in the Lord.

GRACE GIFTS

The gifts of the Spirit are effective in representing the power of God within the church and to unbelievers outside of the church. It is important to understand that while the gifts are mighty in their demonstration, they are not, however, an effective gauge of a person's spiritual development. The gifts are distributed by the grace of God. They can technically be called "grace gifts" because that is their meaning in the original Greek language. This implies that the gifts are not earned or manifested through a person with the intent of validating a person's character or justifying their behavior and lifestyle. Out of the nine spiritual gifts, I think the gift of prophecy has unfortunately been misrepresented the most through individuals who speak forth prophecy but do not live lives that exemplify Christian character.

For instance, Balaam operated in the gift of prophecy but in the eyes of God he was considered to be unrighteous. Balaam had manifestations of the Spirit but he did not have the fruit of the Spirit. The gifts of the Spirit and the fruit of the Spirit are two completely different categories. Let me reemphasize that just because people operate in the gifts of the Spirit does not equate to the fact that they are spiritually mature and are bearing the fruit of righteous living that brings honor and glory to God.

Sometime back, a man in his mid-twenties in age visited my church. While I was preaching, I noticed he got up and left the service about three or four times to use the restroom. After the service was concluded, he asked me in private if he could prophesy to me the word of the Lord. With a few of my ushers standing next to me as witnesses, I said, "Sure, go ahead." He commenced to give me a prophecy that was 100 percent accurate. The prophecy also contained a word of knowledge that there was no possible way he could have naturally known. His gift of prophecy was a confirmation to me of certain things, and I could tell this young man had a prophetic grace upon his life. However, I could also clearly see that this brother in the Lord had addictions in his life that controlled him. His eyes were hazy and he showed obvious indications of someone involved in drug usage.

After this man left the service, the deacons reported to me that someone had been profusely smoking marijuana in the men's restroom. They knew beyond doubt that it had been this particular man. Because this person only visited the church once, the elders and I never had the chance to speak with him again and confront him concerning his sinful behavior. Our church is full of grace, but we also do not sweep sin beneath the carpet nor have the slightest tolerance for illegal activity.

So, here we see an example of a person who could operate accurately in the gift of prophecy and word of knowledge but the fruit of the Spirit was greatly lacking in his life. The fruit of the Spirit is necessary to have so that the gifts of the Spirit are presented in a manner that glorifies the Lord. Gifts are always served best with fresh fruit. The fresh fruit being love, joy, peace, patience, kindness, goodness, faithfulness, gentleness, and self-control.

Some believers have thrown the baby out with the dirty bathwater, in a proverbial sense, to stop the abuse of prophecy. Books have been written about failed prophecies in an effort to bring balance to the misuse of this gift. I myself have received my share of inaccurate prophecies over the years. Misguided prophecies that have been spoken to me never really fazed me because I have a good sense and understanding of God's plan for my life; and if a prophecy doesn't line up with that plan, then I know that it simply missed the mark. It doesn't mean I despise the gift or become upset at the person who gave the prophecy. I just move on and stay focused on what God called me to do.

God really wants His people to have the gift of prophecy. This is the reason why the devil tries so hard to make this gift and those who operate in the gift of prophecy sometimes come across as having the appearance of being weird, strange, or spooky. Honestly, so many of God's own people in the body of Christ reject this precious gift that on occasion I think God has to find the so-called "strange ones" that He can use because the normal folks don't want to be seen prophesying over people. If giving prophecies is considered to be strange or weird, then count me in with that group because I love to prophesy. I cut my teeth in the early days of ministry on prophecy. For instance, I would go to a church, preach a message for about 40 minutes, and then the pastor would line all the church members up and I would prophesy over every single person. It was normal to have services where I would preach and then prophesy over 200 people. It would usually take about an hour to prophesy to 100 people. I did this for years and years before I ever received the healing gifts that expanded my ministry into a broader dimension.

But he who prophesies speaks edification and exhortation and comfort to men (1 Corinthians 14:3).

The basic gift of prophecy is designed by God to build up, encourage, and comfort the people of God. Everybody needs encouragement from time to time. Prophecy gives fresh strength to all who hear this gift in operation. Basic prophecy does not involve any foretelling of future events. When prophecy comes forth through a prophet, it functions on a higher level and it often speaks of future events.

> And in these days prophets came from Jerusalem to Antioch. Then one of them, named Agabus, stood up and showed by the Spirit that there was going to be a great famine throughout all the world, which also happened in the days of Claudius Caesar (Acts 11:27-28).

In this example we see that the prophet Agabus gave a prophecy that contained revelation concerning future events that came to pass exactly as he foretold. It is possible for any believer to give a prophecy that foretells future events, but a prophet will have this manifestation on a much more regular basis. In my own prophetic ministry there are times when a strong gift of prophecy comes upon me.

In 2006, I was ministering locally here in the county in which I live. A Baptist pastor attended one of my conferences that I held that year. He enjoyed my ministry, so he invited me to come to his church and hold several meetings. In the meetings that we were conducting, I was able to lead the Baptist pastor into the baptism of the Holy Spirit, and he began to immediately speak in tongues. The Holy Spirit moved upon me and I prophesied before the congregation that the pastor would be given a new church building, and that it would happen within the time frame of one year. After the meeting was over, my wife later told me what I had said when I gave the prophetic word to the pastor. When I was under the anointing, I was hardly aware of what I was saying because the prophecy was flowing out of me so quickly. When my wife told me of what I had prophesied, I was completely unaware that I spoke that it would happen within a year, but it was recorded on audio disc. Exactly one year went by and Pastor Mike from the Baptist church called me on my cell phone.

Pastor Mike told me that on the 52nd week after I gave that prophecy, he happened to be attending a small convention of Baptist pastors. He was scheduled to speak a message that day at the church that was hosting the convention. He preached a good sermon and then walked down from the pulpit to go sit down. While he was walking toward a seat, another local pastor from here in the county approached him and handed him a set of keys and said, "While you were preaching God told me to give you my church building. I am retiring from ministry and the building is debt free—not a penny is owed on it. You can also assimilate my church members into your church family if they would like to stay." Pastor Mike received the fulfillment of his prophetic word and it happened just a few days before a full year was completed from the date I prophesied it. Since then I have had the pleasure of ministering in his new building numerous times.

The gift of prophecy allows us to dream big and expect a bright future. A true prophecy from God will always bear witness with your spirit—your inner self. At the same time in which a genuine prophecy feels velvety smooth and agreeable with your heart, you can also feel stretched further than you ever thought possible. God is a big God, and He wants us to dream with Him without limits when it comes to where He desires to take us.

So don't be surprised if God takes you out to view the sky on a clear and starry night in order to deposit a personal prophetic promise within your heart. Hold fast to the prophecies you have received from the Lord while knowing that they will come to pass at the right time. Seek the Lord for the gift of prophecy with a fiery passion. The Lord will surely reward you with this gift that has such a unique way of inspiring those who were formerly downtrodden and discouraged to now look up and reach for the stars.

10

MESSAGES FROM GOD TO HIS PEOPLE

But the manifestation of the Spirit is given to each one for the profit of all...to another different kinds of tongues, to another the interpretation of tongues (1 Corinthians 12:7,10).

When many believers think about tongues and interpretation, the image that comes to mind first is someone speaking in a tongue and then another person interpreting the meaning of the tongue. This is a biblical concept, but tongues and interpretation can be so much more than simply this one dimension of operation. Anytime you speak in tongues, you are speaking mysteries to God that only He understands, unless the Holy Spirit unveils the meaning.

In 1998 I was attending a Christian businessmen's annual convention. Before the first session started, there was a group of about 30 of us gathered together to pray for the convention. We were all praying in tongues, there was no one praying in English or in another foreign language. As we were praying, one believer suddenly had understanding of everything another man was uttering in tongues. The man who had understanding began to interpret in English what the other man was saying in tongues. It was wonderful to hear the interpretation of what this man was uttering as he prayed. Much of what was being spoken was actually a heavenly verbal form of praise, worship, and exaltation of the goodness of God.

Seeing and hearing this event take place helped me further understand that praying in tongues is truly a spiritual language. Although our natural minds do not understand the nature of what is being prayed, our inward self is directly communicating with God. Anytime you pray in tongues you are stepping over into the realm of glory. The more time you spend speaking in other tongues, the deeper your experiences with God in the glory realm will become.

Two Types of Tongues

There are two primary types of tongues. First, there is a private gift of tongues that is available for every believer for their own personal edification. This gift is received when a believer is filled with the Holy Spirit. When you speak in tongues you strengthen yourself inwardly as if you were charging a battery. Speaking in tongues regularly to build up spiritual strength is important. Throughout each day I speak in tongues quietly under my breath as I go about my regular activities. This keeps me refreshed and sensitive to the Holy Spirit. Tongues are so important that Apostle Paul devoted almost an entire chapter (1 Corinthians 14) to addressing the various insights into understanding the purpose for tongues, the benefits that the believer gains through speaking in tongues, and the order of a public worship service when tongues and interpretation are in manifestation.

Second, there is a public gift of tongues that is given in a public service to bless the church. When this gift comes forth, it requires an interpretation in order to be productive. The public gift of tongues is the type of tongue mentioned as a spiritual gift in First Corinthians 12:10. When the gift of tongues is in operation, it is basically a message from God to those in the meeting. When I speak in tongues for my own personal edification, I can do this at any time of day or night that I desire. But I cannot speak in the public gift of tongues unless the Holy Spirit moves upon me to function in this gift. Some believers have told me that tongues no longer exist in the church and they cite the following verse to support their belief:

> *Are all apostles? Are all prophets? Are all teachers? Are all workers of miracles? Do all have gifts of healings? Do all speak with tongues? Do all interpret?* (1 Corinthians 12:29-30)

The obvious answer to each of all Paul's questions is "no." Do all speak with tongues? The answer is no. Do all interpret? Again, the answer is no. What some believers have failed to understand, however, is that the tongues and interpretation mentioned by Paul in this verse is not referring to personal use, but rather to ministry use. In other words, the tongues and interpretation is here speaking about two of the nine spiritual gifts that would be used in a setting of a public meeting. Not every believer is called to be an apostle or prophet. Likewise, not every believer is given the spiritual gift of tongues and interpretation of tongues. The ministry gifts (apostles, prophets, evangelists, pastors, and teachers) and the spiritual gifts (the nine which we are studying) are given by the Holy Spirit as He wills. While any believer can have a public tongue and interpretation come forth by the manifestation of the Spirit, certain ministers have this gift operate in their lives frequently as part of the supernatural equipment that goes along with their call to a full-time ministry office.

Concerning the first type of speaking in tongues that we have looked at which is for personal use, every believer can speak in this manner of tongues when they are filled with the Holy Spirit. You can also interpret your own tongues by the Holy Spirit in your personal prayer time.

> *Therefore let him who speaks in a tongue pray that he may interpret* (1 Corinthians 14:13).

There are times when you want to know what it is that you are praying about when you pray in tongues. Your natural mind does not understand but would like to be informed as to what is transpiring. You can understand your spiritual prayer language by asking the Lord to give you the interpretation so that your mind can know what you have been praying about. When you pray in tongues during your personal prayer time, you do not always have to interpret your prayers. Only during certain times when you feel in your heart that it would be good to have the understanding, do you need to seek God for the interpretation.

To interpret your private prayers that are uttered in tongues, just ask the Lord to give you the interpretation through the Holy Spirit. Then, by faith, be still and allow the interpretation to come to you. For me, the interpretation will come as a few words then become a few sentences and usually end up being about a paragraph long—unless the interpretation then merges into prophecy. If it turns into prophecy, then I just speak that out under the anointing of the Holy Spirit. At other times when I pray in tongues, the interpretation of what I am praying about will just float up from inside me and become understood by my mind. Often I receive the interpretation of my tongues without even asking God for the interpretation. This is frequently how I interpret tongues in a public setting. When someone speaks forth a message in the gift of tongues and the interpretation instantly comes to me, then I publicly share the interpretation I received. It's always nice when the interpretation comes before you even have the chance to ask for it.

God does not call everybody to speak in the gift of tongues that is used in a public church meeting, so don't feel that if you receive this gift you will be forced by God to stand before a congregation and speak out a message in tongues. When the gift of tongues comes forth for public edification, you will find that the tongue which is being spoken is sharp, concise, and flows like an uninterrupted stream out of the mouth of the speaker. The interpretation, whether from the speaker or someone else in the meeting, will also come with clarity and concise meaning.

Interpretation is not the same thing as translation. Translation is converting the literal meaning of the words over into another language. However, interpretation is different in that you are expressing the spirit and essence of the message and revealing that spiritual message to the church in a known language, such as English, that the congregation can understand. This is why a person can operate in the gift of tongues and speak out a public message in tongues that may only last for twenty seconds, but the interpretation that follows may last for two minutes. The message needs to be interpreted, not translated. When the interpretation of tongues comes forth, the whole church is uplifted and blessed. Tongues and interpretation bring power and revelation into the church and keep it from becoming dry and stagnant. Tongues can also be seen as a miraculous sign to unbelievers.

> In the law it is written: "With men of other tongues and other lips I will speak to this people; and yet, for all that, they will not hear Me," says the Lord. Therefore tongues

are for a sign, not to those who believe but to unbelievers; but prophesying is not for unbelievers but for those who believe (1 Corinthians 14:21-22).

We see in the second chapter of the book of Acts that when the early Christian disciples were filled with the Holy Spirit, they spoke in tongues and uttered foreign languages that were understood by people of other nations. This happened during the Feasts of Pentecost. Judaism came to regard Pentecost as the anniversary of the giving of the old covenant and law at Mount Sinai. The Pentecostal experience signified the major shift that the believer is now righteous in Christ and not reliant upon the keeping of the law to be justified. Pentecost was one of the seven annual feasts celebrated by the Israelites. The Jewish historian, Flavius Josephus, tells us that during the Feast of Pentecost the city of Jerusalem could see as many as three million attendees consisting of Jews and proselytes (Gentiles who converted to Judaism) from all parts of the world. That's an amazing amount of people—we can only imagine how busy the priests must have been at the Temple. When God poured out His Spirit upon the disciples and they began to speak fluently in foreign tongues, He timed it so that it would have maximum impact upon the massive crowd.

Then they were all amazed and marveled, saying to one another, "Look, are not all these who speak Galileans? And how is it that we hear, each in our own language in which we were born? Parthians and Medes and Elamites, those dwelling in Mesopotamia, Judea and Cappadocia, Pontus and Asia, Phrygia and Pamphylia, Egypt and the parts of Libya adjoining Cyrene, visitors from Rome, both Jews and proselytes, Cretans and Arabs—we hear them speaking in our own tongues the wonderful works of God."

So they were all amazed and perplexed, saying to one another, "Whatever could this mean?" (Acts 2:7-12)

In this instance tongues were used as a miraculous sign to point people to faith in Jesus Christ. The visitors could hear the disciples speaking in their native language the wonderful works of God. Those who received Jesus as their Savior because of the amazing witness brought forth by the gift of tongues then carried their salvation back with them to their home country once the Feast of Pentecost was completed. Thus the gospel began to go beyond Jerusalem and then spread throughout the earth. The gift of tongues as a miraculous sign can be very effective in winning over lost souls to Christ. The Holy Spirit still uses tongues as a miracle sign to unbelievers so that they may hear the good news of Christ through a supernatural format that confirms to them that Jesus is the only Savior and Lord.

It is important that we have these manifestations of the Spirit in our church gatherings. When you come to meet together, it is important to be prayed up so that you bring something of spiritual value to the body of believers. The gift of tongues and the interpretation of tongues will always be beneficial in stirring up the saints of God to press on toward their heavenly call.

As you seek the Lord, it may be the will of God for you to have the two spiritual gifts of tongues and interpretation for public use. If the Holy Spirit is working within your heart to desire these specific gifts, then ask God in faith that He will bestow them upon you. God will honor your spiritual hunger, and He will surely bless you for wanting to uplift His people by delivering the messages that He sends forth through tongues and their interpretation.

11

WHICH ARE THE BEST GIFTS?

But earnestly desire the best gifts (1 Corinthians 12:31).

*But always seek to excel in the greater
gifts...* (1 Corinthians 12:31 WNT).

We are instructed in God's Word to excel or pursue after the greater gifts. The word "excel" in the original Greek language means to "burn with zeal" for the greater gifts. If Paul refers to "greater gifts" then it implies that there are certain gifts that are to be more highly desired than others. The word "greater" can also be translated as "more advantageous" or "more useful." So there are some gifts that we should have a burning desire for because they are more useful and they have a greater advantage over the other gifts.

When considering which gifts would be considered the "best" gifts, we can look at an event that occurred in my life to understand the context that would help us in reaching our decision. In 1996, I was invited by the CEO of the company that I worked for to go out to Nevada for a remote camping experience by the Colorado River. Our company was based in Orange County, California, and Jeff, the boss, thought it would be a fun idea for us to get away from the office and have some time to relax after a very busy spring season. Along with Ron, another senior management official, we rented a motor home, packed up our camping gear and headed out for the five-hour drive from southern California to southern Nevada to see the rugged 1,450 mile Colorado River, known as "America's River."

Being on the adventurous side, we decided to find a remote area of the river that would be unpopulated. We each enjoyed the outdoor environment so once we arrived, we set up camp and relaxed around the campfire as evening soon arrived. Because there were no city lights near our campsite, we could see thousands of brilliant stars at night with the occasional meteor shooting across the darkened sky. We went to bed that night in our sleeping bags with expectation and looked forward to the next day to further explore the area.

In the morning when I woke up, I decided to go for a hike up into the surrounding mountains. The area in which we were camping near the Colorado River was in the Mojave Desert, which covers a large portion of the southern part of Nevada. The Mojave Desert is an extreme place to be because it receives less than 13 inches of rain a year and temperatures in the summer can rise to over 130 degrees. There was a beautiful mountain range rising up from the basin of the river that had an initial ridge with an elevation of about 2,000 feet. If I were to climb the walls of the ridge and reach the top, I thought it would be a good opportunity to possibly see the elusive Desert Bighorn Ram.

That morning, my two friends decided to just hang around the camp. They said that maybe later in the day they might do a little kayaking down the river. So I bid them farewell and announced I would be back in about two hours. With a small backpack and a supply of only 20 ounces of water, I began my ascent by walking up a steep hill that would carry me into a jagged narrow pass that gradually escalated toward the top plateau. The morning temperature was cool because the sun had not yet come over the ridge. It was only about 85 degrees Fahrenheit, and I was confident my physical condition would hold up for a brief two-hour hike.

As my journey continued upward I kept finding new rock crevices that were large enough to work my way through without having to make any risky vertical climbs. However, after an hour of nonstop climbing, I realized the temperature was quickly rising and I had already consumed half of my water. I reassured myself that the hike would be completed within an hour and that the proverbial saying of "It's always faster coming down" would prove to be true once I got to the top. As I continued my climb, the sun eventually came over the ridge and the temperature quickly rose to 100 degrees. Sweating profusely I pressed on, determined to reach the top that I could see was now getting closer. Working my way up through a very steep passage that was as narrow as the eye of a needle, I finally reached the top of the plateau and rejoiced in my accomplishment. The view was spectacular as I could see in an easterly direction for many miles. Far below I could see the Colorado River slowly winding its way through the barren but picturesque landscape.

After walking on the plateau for about ten minutes, I knew I had to return immediately because the searing heat was becoming very difficult to deal with. Looking at my watch I became aware that I had lost track of time and it was now a few minutes after 12 o'clock noon. By now I had been gone for over two hours, so it was time to head back to my campsite. As I endeavored to retrace my steps on the plateau back to the same path that I came up, it became apparent that I had gotten myself somehow turned around and I was unable to find the place where I originally arrived. The more I looked for my pathway down, the more disoriented I became as to where I began.

The plateau offered no shade from the full sun that was now upon me and the effects of heat exhaustion were beginning to affect me so that I could not think clearly. Unable to find my original path, I was forced to explore a new way down. Everywhere I looked there was no easy route down. Steep vertical drop-offs that plunged for hundreds of feet were on both sides of the plateau. Walking a little further on the plateau I noticed a rocky path that appeared to offer the possibility of a less hazardous route.

As I began to carefully descend, I quickly could tell that it was going to be much more difficult getting down than it was coming up. Some places I could climb down by placing my hands on jagged rocks that offered good holds. But other places offered very little to grab on to, and I certainly wasn't skilled in free climbing the sides of mountains. By this time my water was gone, and I could tell my body was becoming dehydrated. The desert temperature rose to 130 degrees and the sun was directly overhead with no shade to escape the blazing heat.

Descending down the almost vertical face of the mountain ridge, I eventually reached a specific spot where there were no footholds to stand on or rocks to grab hold of. I was left with two options. First, I could reverse my climb and go back up from where I came and start over somewhere else. But I was too fatigued to consider this option. Second, I could take a crazy risk and jump with all my strength and hopefully reach a protruding boulder that rested just below me and seemed to be about 8 feet away on my left side. While 8 feet may not seem very far away, it looked very far to me because I had to jump sideways from a standing position. But because I would also be jumping downward, I thought that I could possibly make it. If

I didn't make it, I would surely fall to my death. I decided to take the jump.

Leaping with all my might I surprised myself and cleared the front part of the boulder. The off-balanced landing caused my feet to come down awkwardly on the back side of the boulder. I had actually jumped a little farther than I anticipated but now my forward momentum was carrying me over the back side of the boulder that was sloped inward toward the mountain. With desperation I tried to grab hold of any rough object to stop my fall, but the boulder was as smooth as glass. Sliding uncontrollably I slipped off the boulder and dropped about 10 feet into a hidden cleft within the side of the mountain. Hitting the ground with a solid thud, my body fell to the floor. As I slowly looked up, I noticed I was contained within a small reclusive hollow that was shielded by a wall of surrounding rock that stood about 10 feet high. There in front of me I also saw an amazing sight. The complete skeletal remains of a huge Desert Bighorn Ram lay before me. The skull and horns were in perfect condition, having been preserved by the desert environment that doesn't contain the slightest amount of moisture in the air.

As I lay there on the floor in this hidden cleft of the rock in the remote Mojave Desert, I could tell that the cooling mechanisms in my body were failing to operate. I was no longer sweating, my heart was beating at a rapid rate, and I was struggling not to lose consciousness—all signs of advanced heat stroke, which are deadly if I did not get myself cooled off quickly.

Laying there I realized that if I died in this spot it would be almost impossible for anyone to find me. I thought about this really wonderful woman named Kelly I had met only two weeks earlier. We had hit it off really well and the relationship was definitely going in the right direction. I thought about the possibilities of ministry and what might happen in my life if I were to live and one day preach the gospel. Up until that point in my life I had never really accomplished anything. Most of my time had been spent living for myself and just going through the basic motions of life. But the thought of a happy marriage, the possibility of having children and the distant thought that maybe God could one day work through me to have some type of effective ministry compelled me to get up off that floor. *I've got to keep going,* I told myself with renewed determination.

With weak hands and legs that struggled to say coordinated, I scaled the 10 foot wall of rock and then began working my way once again down the side of the canyon wall. Although there was still no shade I could see the river only about 100 yards directly below. If I could just make it to the edge of the river, I knew I could get refreshed because even in the summer the waters of the Colorado River are a brisk 42 degrees cold. This time I found plenty of good places to grab on to as I slowly lowered myself down the near vertical face of the mountain into a narrow canyon through which the river flowed. Finally I reached the last little ledge and jumped the remaining 4 feet to the ground, which was only a few feet from the bank of the river. I got on my knees and carefully reached both hands into the fast-moving waters of the river. The water was unbelievably cold and refreshing and for the first time a slight shade now hung over me because the sun had moved and was not able to reach into the lowest part of the canyon.

With great relief I took big handfuls of water and slowly drank them and threw the cool water over the rest of my body. I had to be careful because the bank of the river was only a 2-foot-wide ledge of rock, and I was trapped next to the river and the base of the inner-canyon wall. The river dropped off to an immediate depth of 20 feet and there was no way in my condition that I had any strength to swim. I simply lay down and slowly kept placing handfuls of water on my body, which was gradually beginning to recover from heat exhaustion.

After laying there for about 30 minutes I sat up and wondered how I was going to get off of the rock ledge that was positioned next to the deep-water river in such an isolated location. To my surprise I faintly began to hear voices talking just around the bend of the river. After a few minutes I watched as two kayaks and their paddlers appeared floating around the corner—Ron and Jeff!

"Hey Steven, what are you doing here?" they asked when they saw me. With a smile of relief and elation I said, "I'm just hanging out, and looking for a ride to get off of this rock." Jeff paddled over and gave me a ride back to our campsite. Along the way Jeff and Ron actually pulled me through the water while I held on to their kayaks. Completely submerging my entire body in the cold water helped to reduce the effects of the heat stroke, although it took me a few days to get back to normal after having had such a close call with death.

THE CHOICE OF GIFTS

In light of our study of which spiritual gifts are the best gifts, I think back on the story I just shared. While lying on the floor in the cleft of the rock, what would I have done if someone appeared to me at that time and said, "I have come to offer you the choice of two gifts. You can either have a gallon of cool water, or you can have a large bag full of diamonds, rubies, and sapphires." Without hesitation I would have chosen the gallon of water because it was clearly the gift that was most needed at that particular time. The Holy Spirit knows which gifts are needed at critical times and He is able to manifest those gifts to those in need. So from one perspective, we can reason that the best gift is the one that is most needed at that specific time.

Our Scripture reference tells us to desire the best gifts, placing an emphasis upon the plurality of certain gifts. This would indicate that there are still specific gifts that are to be more highly preferred over others. In other words, suppose everything in your life is going along fine and you do not need a miracle through supernatural intervention or any particular gift to be manifested. Let's assume you are offered the ability of being able to pick any of the nine gifts and have one manifested on your behalf. Which one would you choose?

When we look closely at the three categories of spiritual gifts, there is a clear distinction regarding the ones that stand at the forefront. In order to determine which gifts are best, we must take a brief look at the three different categories that comprise the spiritual gifts. The nine spiritual gifts can be separated into three categories:

1. Revelation Gifts

2. Power Gifts

3. Vocal Gifts

The revelation gifts are manifested by the Holy Spirit in order to reveal something by the Spirit of God. The three revelation gifts are the word of wisdom, word of knowledge, and discerning of spirits. The power gifts are mighty manifestations of the Holy Spirit that accomplish something for the glory of God. The three power gifts are faith, healings, and working of miracles. There are three vocal gifts that are each expressed through what we say, and those three gifts include prophecy, tongues, and the interpretation of tongues.

In each of the three categories there is a specific gift that stands on a higher level than the others. In the revelation gifts, the *word of wisdom* is the best gift because it reveals God's precise purpose and plan for someone's life. This gift may not appear to be spectacular when it manifests, but the results of obeying the Holy Spirit when this gift comes forth can prove to be truly miraculous and deeply gratifying.

The *gift of faith* is the best gift in the category of the power gifts. Many times believers ask God for the gift of working of miracles because this gift is amazing to see in demonstration. But what many believers fail to understand is that super faith is always in manifestation when a person operates in the gift of working of miracles. When the gifts of healings are operating in my life, I always sense that super faith is in manifestation as well. So the power gift that is to your best advantage is the *gift of super faith*. If you want to operate strongly in the power gifts, you must ask God for the gift of super faith to be given to you. This gift will cause healings and miracles to follow you.

The vocal gifts are beautiful in their expression. The gift of tongues and interpretation can be quite dramatic when in full manifestation. This is a gift that unless it is seen in manifestation can often be tricky for a believer to realize just how effective it is in opening our awareness to God's supernatural power. But out of the three vocal gifts, it is the *gift of prophecy* that has the edge as being the best gift. Prophecy has many different levels of which it can be administered to others, and it is a gift that is so easy for any believer to move into. Even believers who are young in the faith can find this gift bubbling up and wanting to come out in their efforts to share the love of Christ with others. Whether it is the gift coming forth in its simplest form to build up, exhort, and comfort, or if it is the more advanced levels of speaking under a strong unction of the Spirit, the gift of prophecy is the leading vocal gift.

THE BEST OVERALL GIFT

As we look across the spectrum of all nine gifts, is it possible to narrow down one single gift that would be the best overall gift? In my opinion, I believe that the word of wisdom is the best overall gift. Actually, out of the nine gifts mentioned in the twelfth chapter of First Corinthians, the gift that is mentioned first is the word of wisdom. The Lord knows the past, present, and future. When He presents a word of wisdom to you, it is an opportunity to participate in the perfect will of God concerning your life. God wants to steer you in the right direction according to His plan for your life. Your destiny can be deeply affected by this gift. Your life assignment and reason for being sent to this earth can be furthered through this gift. When the word of wisdom is offered to you, it is best to accept it and act upon it as quickly as possible.

Pause and think about the importance of the word of wisdom. Through the word of wisdom God told Noah to build an ark. He told him specific details concerning the type of wood to use, the approximate dimensions, how many levels it would contain, and other fine points so that it would be constructed according to the divine plan. About the only thing God did not tell Noah was a date of when the coming flood would occur. God rarely gives dates because He expects us to walk by faith and stay busy doing what we are supposed to do. Along with Noah, many other Bible characters were launched into their primary life assignments through the word of wisdom.

Abraham was told by the Lord through the word of wisdom to leave his home country and his relatives and go to a land that He would show him. Moses received the word of wisdom to build the tabernacle in the desert. David received the word of wisdom through a prophet concerning the Temple that his son Solomon would build. This prompted David to store up spoils of war so he could contribute greatly toward the costs of the construction of the temple. An angel of God delivered a word of wisdom to the parents of Samson that informed them of his Nazarite calling and holy consecration before he was even born. The list could go on and on of those whose lives were directly influenced by the word of wisdom.

Is there any other gift that is so integral in the initial unveiling and eventual fulfillment of your life purpose other than the gift of the word of wisdom? These examples are why I believe the gift of the word of wisdom is the best gift.

Because of my ministry calling, I place a lot of personal emphasis on developing the gift of faith because this gift is such a tremendous help to me when praying for the sick or for those in need of a miracle. You will find over time that a few specific gifts will become very close to you, and you will want to develop those particular gifts as much as you can. As you walk closely with the Lord, eventually you can develop a relationship with Him where it can appear as if those certain gifts seem to follow you wherever you go.

From a final perspective, it is good to consider that the best gifts could also be viewed as those that the Holy Spirit gives to you personally by His own choosing. God knows what you need in life to fulfill your assignment, so He desires for you to seek Him diligently so that He might supply and make available to you the tools and necessary spiritual gifts in order for you to succeed.

12

Humility to Flow in the Gifts

A sincere desire to move in the gifts of the Holy Spirit must also be combined with a mutual desire to exalt the Lord in all we do. All that we have comes from God. Every talent, every blessing, and every divine gift all have their origin from our gracious Lord Jesus. Whenever the gifts of the Spirit are in operation, it will without question draw attention. When the glory of God is manifested, it is like a radiant light that shines forth, causing others to draw near and behold its brilliance. It is during times like these when we must be extra careful to give all the credit to God. We must firmly resist the temptation to take even one ounce of God's glory for ourselves. We are granted the privilege of being conduits through which God can flow His power. But we must recognize that the power comes from God. We have no intrinsic power or righteousness within ourselves. Outside of Christ—we can do nothing.

If we ever forget to stay humble, we can be assured that the Lord will withdraw His mighty anointing from our lives and the spiritual gifts will become corrupted. We must be careful to steward the glory—not take it for ourselves. Pride is an enemy that we must guard against. Pride has a way of trying to sneak into our lives, especially when the Lord is working through us. These temptations concerning pride often present themselves in their most subtle form when we reach a certain level of success. The gifts are charismatic. In other words, a person who moves in the gifts of the Spirit moves in an anointing that supernaturally attracts attention. The world identifies it as a magnetic charm, or an ability to influence a large number of people.

The spiritual gifts come from God as a divine spiritual endowment. Anything that comes from heaven is going to get noticed. You have to prepare yourself to deal with people who want to put you on a pedestal when the gifts manifest through you. If you allow yourself to become exalted in pride, you will surely fall.

When we examine the lives of biblical characters we see the sobering need to walk in humility before the Lord. Saul had just been anointed by the prophet Samuel to be the king of Israel. When it came time to present the new king to the people during a formal ceremony, they could not find Saul anywhere. God revealed that Saul was hiding among the baggage of all the people who had gathered at Mizpah. Saul knew that God had chosen him, but he was also aware of his own inadequacies, inexperience, and unworthiness. Here we get a glimpse into the initial humility that Saul walked in. Saul acknowledged that he was from the smallest tribe, and from the smallest family in the tribe. There was nothing of himself in which he could boast.

Humility was a key quality that caught God's attention and caused the kingdom to be placed into Saul's hands. There was much to learn for Saul. Israel never had a king before. The protocol of royal behavior had to be taught to the people by Samuel. Saul had no former training on how to run a government. He did not graduate from a military academy where officers are taught the ground rules of warfare. A war with the Ammonites was looming and Saul was quickly placed in a position of either sink or swim.

It would be like you or I going to a new job on the first day. It takes a while to process and learn all of the new things that are being thrown at you. Only after a few months do you begin to feel a little comfortable and confident in knowing what to do. This was a humble time for Saul. He needed instruction and advice to learn how to function in his new capacity. He was greatly reliant upon God's help.

For a brief period of time Saul proved to be a successful leader and collected several military victories. But it only took about two years for Saul to get himself into trouble by not obeying the full commands of God. After a time of success his confidence in himself soared and his reliance upon God plummeted. Saul disobeyed a direct command of God and was rejected by God as king. The prophet Samuel was sent to Gilgal with a message revealing God's judgment to Saul.

So Samuel said, "When you [Saul] were little in your own eyes, were you not head of the tribes of Israel? And did not the Lord anoint you king over Israel?" (1 Samuel 15:17)

There are different ways of viewing success. God views people as being successful not by how they begin, but how they finish. In other words, it's not how you start a race, but how you finish that counts. At the beginning of a race everyone looks good. Halfway through a race many runners continue to look good. But you can't win if you don't finish. When you walk in humility, you will avoid the majority of pitfalls that keep many good runners from crossing the finish line.

This may surprise you, but in the Bible we see a pattern of repetition that occurs with the nation of Israel and many of its leaders. The disturbing pattern is that the people of God do not generally fall when faced with trails, difficulties, or great challenges. Rather, they are most prone to failure when having reached a place of success. King Saul became arrogant after achieving victories over the Ammonites and Philistines. His pride resulted in his downfall. The last night of his life was spent in consultation with a witch and his final day ended with him committing suicide.

David became king after going through a great development period in which he faced unusual hardships. God raised up a humble shepherd boy to take the throne of Israel, much to the delight of His people. He was doing exceptionally well until he abandoned a position of humility and began to drift away from the Lord. The next thing you know he had seduced Bathsheba into an adulterous affair and then goes on to plot the murder of her husband in an effort to conceal his sin. He fell when he had reached a place of success. David repented and God restored him, but he paid a heavy price for his sins.

Solomon had two personal visitations from the Lord. He came on the scene with deep humility, knowing within his heart that he did not possess the qualities necessary to govern such a mighty nation. Because of his humble request, God gave him wisdom and understanding to lead the nation into what became known as the "Golden Age" of Israel. But during the height of his success Solomon also fell away from the Lord. His foreign wives (whom God told him not to marry) turned his heart away from the Lord, and the once humble king hardened his heart with pride and worshiped the gods Baal, Ashtoreth, and Milcom.

Before he died Solomon returned to the Lord. The book of Ecclesiastes was written by him after having turned from idolatry. However, even after repentance, his sin had opened the door for much evil to gain entrance into the land of Israel. Shortly after Solomon's death, the nation was divided. The northern kingdom was a complete failure, with each successive king delving deeply into idolatry and occultism.

The southern kingdom had a few good kings every now and then, but the majority of them were not loyal to the Lord.

SELF-DEPENDENCE

Pride can be described as "self-dependence." Humility is reliance upon the mercy of God, knowing that without Him we can do nothing. Our talents, our gifting, our intellect, our natural abilities all come from God. Every good and perfect gift is from the Heavenly Father. When we tell God that He is our strength, our empowerment, our all in all, then we place ourselves in a safe position. The Hebrew word for "humble" means "to be low." When we lose our humility, we develop a "big head" that causes us to be lifted up in pride. When we are lifted up in arrogance, we bang our head into hard objects that could otherwise be avoided. If we remain humble, we fly low and operate in stealth mode. This makes it hard for the enemy to find us on his radar. Prideful people make easy targets for the devil to shoot down.

Pride goes before destruction, and a haughty spirit before a fall (Proverbs 16:18).

One of my favorite characters in the Bible is King Uzziah. Every time I read about his life I marvel at how much God blessed him. We all desire to have God's blessing working in our lives. Uzziah had the blessing functioning in his life in a remarkable degree. It appeared that everything he touched was blessed by God. The Scriptures tell us that Uzziah excelled in many areas until he stumbled in his pride. His life's example is another lesson for us to consider when we look at the temptations that come when success is being experienced. Please consider the following verses that demonstrate the tremendous level of blessing Uzziah was walking in before he was struck with leprosy because of his sin.

Uzziah was sixteen years old when he became king, and he reigned fifty-two years in Jerusalem. His mother's name was Jecholiah of Jerusalem. And he did what was right in the sight of the Lord, according to all that his father Amaziah had done. He sought God in the days of Zechariah, who had understanding in the visions of God; and as long as he sought the Lord, God made him prosper (2 Chronicles 26:3-5).

God helped him against the Philistines, against the Arabians who lived in Gur Baal, and against the Meunites. Also the Ammonites brought tribute to Uzziah. His fame spread as far as the entrance of Egypt, for he became exceedingly strong (verses 7-8).

And Uzziah built towers in Jerusalem at the Corner Gate, at the Valley Gate, and at the corner buttress of the wall; then he fortified them. Also he built towers in the desert. He dug many wells, for he had much livestock, both in the lowlands and in the plains; he also had farmers and vinedressers in the mountains and in Carmel, for he loved the soil (verses 9-10).

And he made devices in Jerusalem, invented by skillful men, to be on the towers and the corners, to shoot arrows and large stones. So his fame spread far and wide, for he was marvelously helped till he became strong (verse 15).

But when he was strong his heart was lifted up, to his destruction, for he transgressed against the Lord his God by entering the temple of the Lord to burn incense on the altar of incense. So Azariah the priest went in after him, and with him were eighty priests of the Lord—valiant men. And they withstood King Uzziah, and said to him, "It is not for you, Uzziah, to burn incense to the Lord, but for the priests, the sons of Aaron, who are consecrated to burn incense. Get out of the sanctuary, for you have trespassed! You shall have no honor from the Lord God." Then Uzziah became furious; and he had a censer in his hand to burn incense. And while he was angry with the priests, leprosy broke out on his forehead, before the priests in the house of the Lord, beside the incense altar. And Azariah the chief priest and all the priests looked at him, and there, on his forehead, he was leprous; so they thrust him out of that place. Indeed he also hurried to get out, because the Lord had struck him. King Uzziah was a leper until the day of his death. He dwelt in an isolated house, because he was a leper; for he was cut off from the house of the Lord (verses 16-21).

Every good gift we have has come down to us from our Father in heaven. We should always be mindful to thank Him for every gift He has placed into our lives. Too many times God's own people do not give Him proper credit for the unique gifts they have received from Him. Whether it's the ability to sing like an angel, function with intelligence like Albert Einstein, or play the violin like a virtuoso by the age of twelve, we must realize that all of these talents are put into us by God. He is the author of life. Every good thing originates from Him. Because it comes from Him, how then can we take the credit? Someone may respond by saying, "Well, He gave me the gift of singing with a beautiful voice, but I developed the gift through much training. Therefore I should receive the glory." But God is the one who also places inside us the will and desire to train and practice. Without the factor of motivation, we wouldn't even have a desire to get out of bed in the morning.

King David was a person who gave significantly toward the building of the Temple. His son Solomon built the Temple, but David contributed largely to making sure that when the time came to build that there would be ample finances and material resources in place for the work. David's generous heart greatly prompted the other Jews to also give sacrificially toward the building project. David mentions that he gave from his own personal funds 3,000 talents of gold. In today's economy the current price for an ounce of gold is $1,800. One talent is equal to 75 pounds. There are 16 ounces in a pound. Therefore 3,000 talents would be today's equivalent of over $60 billion. David was a king, psalmist, warrior, prophet, and also a multibillionaire. He also gave, in today's monetary value, over $250 million in silver. All of those battles he fought over the years in which he acquired spoils were for a divine purpose. Some scholars who study Old Testament history have shared that if the Temple built by Solomon were reconstructed today, it would cost far over one trillion dollars.

When David made the offering for the construction of the Temple, he knew that God was the source of his wealth. With a humble heart we see David openly declare that God is the one who blesses us with wealth. Although David possessed enormous wealth, he did not boast that it was attained due to his own ability or greatness. He gave the credit to God. How many multibillionaires living today would be willing to say the same thing? Here is a portion of David's prayer:

> Both riches and honor come from You, and You reign over all. In Your hand is power and might; in Your hand it is to make great and to give strength to all. "Now therefore, our God, we thank You and praise Your glorious name. But who am I, and who are my people, that we should be able to offer so willingly as this? For all things come from You, and of Your own we have given You" (1 Chronicles 29:12-14).

When we give to God we are simply giving back to Him what He has initially given to us. In the first letter that Apostle Paul wrote to

Timothy he commanded that those who are rich in the present age should not be arrogant or prideful. When people are arrogant because of their wealth, they are blind in realizing that their wealth came from God. Jesus said that the Heavenly Father makes His sun rise on the evil and on the good, and sends rain to fall on the just and on the unjust. Everything that is good comes from God, so we must exercise humility and give God praise for all that He does.

By God's Grace

The gifts of the Holy Spirit are technically called "grace gifts" in the original Greek New Testament. In other words, these gifts operate by God's grace and they are manifested through us not because we earn or deserve them, but simply because God in His sovereignty chooses to work through us. For example, in the earlier years of my ministry I stood in the office of the prophet and teacher. My ministry at that time consisted of teaching the Word of God, and then ministering to the people primarily through the gifts of prophecy, word of knowledge, and discerning of spirits. At times I would pray for sick people because I knew that Jesus said, "they will lay hands on the sick, and they will recover" (Mark 16:18). So, by faith I would pray for the sick, and I saw quite a few people recover from their condition of disease or sickness. However, at that time I did not have a specific anointing to pray for the sick with a grace to operate in the gifts of healings.

This all changed when the Lord Jesus granted to me the anointing to operate in the gifts of healings. The day this gift came I still remember exactly where I was and the moment the gift came upon me. From that point on I knew I possessed something that I did not have before. Overnight, a new dimension of my ministry came forth. Immediately after this I began to pray more consistently for sick people, and there was a dramatic increase in the results. Shortly after receiving this divine gift, I was ministering in a church in California. There was a long line of people who desired prayer after I finished teaching. I started at one end of the line and worked my way down, laying my hands on the people and praying for their healing. There was a tangible anointing present, which means that God's healing power could actually be felt. When I got to the very last person in line, I encountered a young woman who was sixteen years of age. Her entire life had existed with suffering from a severe form of scoliosis of the spine.

This young woman's condition was so acute that she was required to wear a specially designed back brace 22 hours out of every 24-hour day. Just before coming into the healing line she told her mother that she wanted to remove the back brace before receiving prayer. When I came to her, she briefly told me of her condition. I laid my hands on her and in the name of Jesus I rebuked the evil disease of scoliosis and commanded it to completely leave her body. After I prayed for her, she turned around and went back to her seat and told her mother that she believed she was healed. It was as simple as that. No light from heaven shown down on us. No feelings of angel feathers falling on our heads. It was simply her using her faith to connect with the healing gift that God operates through me. Her eyes were totally on the Lord as her Healer, not on me.

Two days later, the pastor of the church in which I had ministered called me. He said the young woman woke up the next morning after I had prayed for her and got out of bed and suddenly noticed her back was completely normal! Her mother came in and also saw the great miracle that had taken place. That same day they had an appointment with the doctor. Her life up to that point had been a continuing journey of traveling back and forth to the doctor for ongoing treatments. The instant she walked into the doctor's office the doctor took one look at her and exclaimed, "Oh my, what has happened to your back!" She smiled and said, "The Lord Jesus has healed me."

The doctor carried out a full examination and to his amazement he verified that the scoliosis was completely gone and she now had a perfectly formed spine. At the conclusion of his examination, the "Brace Specialist" came in to make his weekly adjustment of the brace so that it would be assured of fitting correctly. The head doctor spoke to the specialist as he walked into the room and said, "Sir, your services are no longer needed. This woman's back is now completely well." The mother sent me the full written testimony of her daughter's healing a few weeks after this event took place.

As you can see from this one example, it is apparent that the Lord Jesus gave me a gift that I previously did not have. The Holy Spirit then worked through me and caused this gift to strongly manifest toward the young woman. Jesus healed the woman from scoliosis. Since the gift came from God, was manifested by the Holy Spirit, and was something that was beyond my own ability to do, then how could I possibly take any credit for it? All the credit must go to the Lord Jesus. We are vessels through which He works. But it is He who does the work. When we thank God and give Him the glory for the great things He does, then He sees that we are trustworthy. This makes it possible for the Lord to work through us on a regular basis.

It is possible to be well known and famous yet still be a hard target for the devil to track because of the practice of humility. As you are now coming into a solid understanding and manifestation of the gifts of the Spirit, it's important to always remember what happened to Israel and her kings. Stay humble. Give God the credit and recognition for every good thing that happens when you pray or minister to others.

Be quick to give Him the glory. Let others know that every miracle that occurs comes from the Lord Himself. Whether it is a headache that instantly leaves or a person who leaps out of a wheelchair as you pray, it is important that you be prepared now to give God the glory. As you stay low, you will see that God's grace will lift you to new heights of effective ministry to others, and an increased level of authority will come forth at this time in your life.

13

Unraveling Spiritual Mysteries

As you pursue the spiritual gifts and walk in the fruit of the Spirit, you will begin to merge into a place where you become very sensitive to the leading of the Holy Spirit. This will prove to be a great asset because so many believers are acutely unfamiliar with the ways of God. They often have genuine experiences that God grants them, but they do not grasp the purpose or meaning intended by the experience. They feel like there's no one they can turn to who can answer their questions concerning spiritual matters. They are looking for someone who can help them make sense out of it all. The Lord wants you to be the type of person who can point them in the right direction in their quest to know God.

When you reach a point where the spiritual gifts are in a constant stream that emerges out of you, it is because the Holy Spirit is resting upon your life in a beautiful manner. At this point of spiritual progress, the Holy Spirit will often carry you into a prophetic anointing similar to what the prophet Ezekiel was aware of. This anointing is similar to a river in which some believers enter and stand only in water that is ankle deep. Others venture farther out and arrive at a point that is knee deep, and some progress to the waist-deep level. But if you keep going, you will eventually find that your feet can't touch the bottom anymore. Those who know how to swim in the Spirit are in a qualified position to give "swimming lessons" to those who are just getting into the water for the first time.

> *Again he measured one thousand [cubits], and it was a river that I could not cross; for the water was too deep, water in which one must swim, a river that could not be crossed* (Ezekiel 47:5).

The believer who is spiritually minded is able to go in and out of the glory realm and receive revelation and understanding of the mysteries of God. There are certain messages that the Spirit of the Lord will try to convey to us that are often sent through a form of spiritual code language. If we are not prayerful, then it is possible that we can misunderstand the intended application of the message, or even fail to comprehend its meaning. These messages from God can come through dreams that we know are sent from Him but we are unable to interpret them through our natural understanding. Dreams from God are often conveyed through stories or images that are symbolic in their meaning and thus can only be interpreted correctly by the Holy Spirit.

Along with dreams, there can be life experiences that are so unusual that they require valid prayerful attention to discern their spiritual meaning. The Lord Jesus stands at the head of the five ministry offices that He gave to the church. The five offices are apostle, prophet, evangelist, pastor, and teacher. Jesus is the Prophet who represents the fullness of what the ministry office of the prophet is to be. One thing I've learned over the years is that He can be very prophetic in His actions and in the way that He communicates.

The reason the Lord cloaks certain messages with prophetic code is because He desires for us to mature spiritually to a point where we will seek Him to uncover the answer. This process releases within us the true kingly and prophetic anointing that He desires for us to walk in. Consider the following Scripture:

> *It is the glory of God to conceal a matter, but the glory of kings is to search out a matter* (Proverbs 25:2).

When we search out a matter that is a spiritual mystery to us, we must rely upon the Holy Spirit to unravel or untie the full message that has been sent. For years I used to see the numbers 11-11 on a continual basis, to a point where it seemed like it was being supernaturally impressed before me. Whenever I randomly happened to look at a clock it would say 11:11. Over time the Holy Spirit explained to me that He was using this particular set of numbers to confirm to me that I was walking in His plan for my life and all was well. Those numbers would pop in the most unexpected places and bring an outward confirmation to an inward leading that I felt was of the Lord. The Lord was working to give me a double witness both inwardly by His Holy Spirit and outwardly through these numbers that I was in His perfect will.

My friend Wade Taylor, who has now gone on to heaven, used to have the continual experience of finding a penny every time he was at a specific place where the Lord wanted Him to be. At times we would eat at a restaurant and talk about the goodness of God and discuss certain spiritual topics that we both enjoyed. Once finished with our meal and before getting up to leave, Wade would look on the floor and pick up a lost penny. He would smile and say, "I always find a penny when I am where the Lord wants me to be."

DISTINCT EXPERIENCES

The Lord wants you to be developed in the prophetic flow, but He doesn't want you to be superstitious. I don't seek after signs or phenomena to lead me in my decisions. I base my decisions upon the guidance of God's Word and the leading of the Holy Spirit. The Lord confirms His best for you by throwing in extra confirmations that are unique in corresponding to your walk with Him.

Whenever you have an unusual dream or distinctive experience that you are keenly aware of as having originated from God, but you are left perplexed toward its meaning, then you must be willing to search out the matter. This is when we go to the Lord in prayer and wait until the revelation comes from the Holy Spirit. Daniel had a reputation for explaining things that were hidden beyond the understanding of even the most highly educated men with outstanding intellectual ability. He understood how to wait on the Lord until the Holy Spirit revealed to him the meaning of hidden spiritual truths.

> *Inasmuch as an excellent spirit, knowledge, understanding, interpreting dreams, solving riddles, and explaining enigmas were found in this Daniel, whom the king named Belteshazzar, now let Daniel be called, and he will give the interpretation* (Daniel 5:12).

When Daniel was asked to explain enigmas, in the Hebrew language he was being asked to "untie knots." Recently my daughter handed me a pair of headphones and the cord was all tangled up with several knots. I knew by looking at it that I could untangle it, but it ended up taking me longer than I thought. Unraveling spiritual mysteries can sometimes take a little while—you may have to go one word (knot) at a time until it is all untangled. In the early phases of his prophetic ministry, Daniel would have to pray many hours into the night to get the understanding he needed to solve a spiritual mystery. As he progressed in the prophet's ministry in his latter age, he came to a place where he could on the spot deliver the full interpretation of spiritual dreams, riddles, and word puzzles from God.

Sometimes when I have a dream from God, the full understanding will be there as soon as I wake up. But many other times when God gives me a dream, I don't always know what it means. In these cases I have to search out the meaning by waiting on the Lord with a prayerful heart and letting the Holy Spirit bring the understanding. Often this happens by getting out of bed as soon as the dream is over and going to the living room couch so I can prayerfully meditate. It is not unusual for this to happen at 2 or 4 o'clock in the morning. Of course this is not always easy, but decoding a message from the Lord will bring a deep blessing into your life.

You can't always read a book on the subject of dream interpretation and expect to get all of your answers that way. While good books on this subject can help, you must still rely upon the Holy Spirit to bring forth the accurate interpretation. When Joseph and Daniel interpreted dreams, they often brought forth a meaning that did not match the "rules" of dream interpretation. That's because there are no set rules. Books by Christian authors on dream interpretation are written as supplemental guides to help you understand the basics, but only the Holy Spirit has the complete interpretation.

There can be certain events that take place in your life that are so beyond the possibility of luck or random chance that you *know* God was trying to speak to you through that incident. Don't let a blessing slip past you by failing to understand the meaning for such divine occasions. The Lord could be speaking a warning to you, or He could be endeavoring to confirm you are in His blessed plan. He could be trying to help you avoid trouble, or He could be trying to help you see an open door that He wants you to go through.

Sometimes the Lord is very clear in His instructions and no special prayer is needed, while other times He likes to come with prophetic overtones and present His messages in parables, riddles, or symbolic form which require us to seek Him for the fullness of their meaning. Either way we must be prepared to stay open to the different languages of prophetic communication. You will see a new dimension of the Lord as the Prophet and gain a greater appreciation of His love for you through the messages He will reveal to you.

14

A Special Impartation for You to Flow in the Gifts

It's not an accident that this book has ended up in your hands. As of the year 2013, the Internet search engine company, Google, estimates that there are 130,000,000 books in print (that's one hundred and thirty million!). New statistics show that this number will be doubled within four years! Over 15 million books are expected to be published next year and this number is expected to continue its dramatic increase. Therefore, the chances of this book getting into your hands are a direct expression of God's desire and intent for you to become a person who is skilled and fluent in the gifts of the Holy Spirit. God has divinely orchestrated your steps so that you come into a clear understanding of the spiritual gifts and move accurately in them.

The steps of a good man are ordered by the Lord, and He delights in his way (Psalm 37:23).

God takes delight in the fact that you have chosen to study the spiritual gifts and pursue their manifestation in your life. Gifts are made to be given. God wants to impart to you the spiritual gifts so that you can be a blessing to others with these gifts. As you have read through this book it has been my prayer that you will desire to have an open heart to see the nine gifts of the Spirit operate in your life. As you have pondered the nine gifts, there have probably been a few particular ones that seemed to stand out to you with significance. These special gifts that captivate your heart the most are the gifts that the Holy Spirit would desire to have you operate in. It is possible to have all nine gifts operate in your life on different occasions over time. But there will be certain ones that can be frequent, consistent, and dependable that you become highly developed in using.

> *For I long to see you, that I may impart to you some spiritual gift, so that you may be established* (Romans 1:11).

You will certainly enjoy having the gifts operate in your life; but the primary purpose for the gifts operating through you, is to glorify Jesus and strengthen and establish others in the faith. The spiritual gifts build faith in the hearts of God's people and inspire them to serve God fervently. The gifts capture the attention of those who are lost and without Christ, and give strong cause for them to move toward placing their faith in the Lord Jesus as their Savior. Apostle Paul prayed for Timothy and released an impartation for him to excel in ministry and for the gift of God to be expressed through him.

> *Therefore I remind you to stir up the gift of God which is in you through the laying on of my hands* (2 Timothy 1:6).

Do not neglect the gift that is in you, which was given to you by prophecy with the laying on of the hands of the eldership (1 Timothy 4:14).

As you have been reading the pages of this book, the Holy Spirit has been imparting to you an understanding of the gifts that He is going to give you. Once a gift is given to you by God, then it is yours to keep for the rest of your life. After having received it, if you ever feel the gift has lost its edge, then you need to bump up your prayer life and include a little fasting to once again sharpen your ability to effectively use the gift. The gift will always operate as long as you honor the Lord and live a life that is yielded to the Holy Spirit.

For the gifts and calling of God are without repentance (Romans 11:29 KJV).

At this time I would like to pray for you to receive the gifts that the Holy Spirit wants to give you. As a sign of your humility toward God I would ask that you find a quiet place where you can kneel down and receive this blessing from the Lord. Please pray the following prayer to your Heavenly Father.

Heavenly Father, I thank You for the Holy Spirit who gives the nine spiritual gifts. Thank You for sending the Holy Spirit into the earth to be my Counselor, Comforter, and my Best Friend. Lord Jesus, You were the supreme example of a man who was yielded to the Father's will and filled with the Spirit. Your life and ministry were successful because of Your willingness to follow the leading of the Holy Spirit. Lord, You have instructed me in Your Word to desire spiritual gifts. In obedience to Your Word I seek after You for the best gifts. Let my life be yielded unto You in such a way that You are able to flow Your mighty power through me. At this time I ask that You fill me to overflowing with Your Holy Spirit, and that the gifts You have for me will be released and now begin to operate in my life. Lord God, I worship You. By faith I now receive the gifts that You have chosen for me. Thank You, Father, thank You, Lord Jesus, and thank You, Holy Spirit.

While you are on your knees before the Lord, I want to speak an impartation into your life:

Heavenly Father, may this person reading this right now be blessed by You to operate in the spiritual gifts. I thank You, Father, that You have heard his or her prayer and that right now the spiritual gifts are being stirred within this person. I ask that You give this believer opportunities to use the gifts You are now releasing. I pray for the reader that you grant boldness to step out into the gifts by faith as Your Spirit moves. I pray that You grant to the reader a sensitivity to Your Spirit and a tender heart of compassion to reach out to the hurting and suffering souls with the love and power of the resurrected Christ. Thank You, Lord, for a heavenly impartation into the very heart of the reader—right now! In the name of Jesus, amen.

Now that you have received an impartation from the Lord, it is important to look for those opportunities that will allow you to minister to others with the spiritual gifts. The more you step out in faith and exercise the spiritual gifts, the more comfortable you will feel and the sharper you will be in its implementation. It's very similar to strength training in that the more consistent you are with your training, the stronger you become. There are times when I step out and pray for people when there is no anointing and no manifestation of the Spirit. But when I step out in an effort to bless someone who is in need, the Holy Spirit will come because God honors faith, and our faith should always work by love.

The Lord has imparted to you spiritual gifts. Now go and walk in the power of the Spirit and reveal the love of Christ to those whom God places in your daily path. May your life reflect the beauty and glory of the Lord as His Spirit moves through you.

Prayer to Receive Salvation in Jesus Christ and the Infilling of the Holy Spirit

Perhaps you came across this book and have not yet had the opportunity to personally receive Jesus Christ as Savior and Lord. I invite you to open your heart to Him now. Please read the following verses from the Bible out loud. When you vocalize Bible verses, it allows bold faith to enter into your heart.

> Seek the Lord while He may be found, call upon Him while He is near. Let the wicked forsake his way, and the unrighteous man his thoughts; let him return to the Lord, and He will have mercy on him; and to our God, for He will abundantly pardon (Isaiah 55:6-7).

> All of us have become like one who is unclean, and all our righteous acts are like filthy rags; we all shrivel up like a leaf, and like the wind our sins sweep us away (Isaiah 64:6 NIV).

For God loved the world so much that he gave his one and only Son, so that everyone who believes in him will not perish but have eternal life (John 3:16 NLT).

And it shall come to pass that whoever calls on the name of the Lord shall be saved (Acts 2:21).

There is salvation in no one else! God has given no other name under heaven by which we must be saved (Acts 4:12 NLT).

For all have sinned and fall short of the glory of God (Romans 3:23).

If you confess with your mouth that Jesus is Lord and believe in your heart that God raised him from the dead, you will be saved (Romans 10:9 NLT).

Now that you have read how you may be saved, you can obey the Word of God and make your life right with God. Simply pray the following prayer from your heart with sincerity, and Jesus will give you His eternal life.

Dear Lord Jesus, today I choose to make You my Lord and Savior. I confess that You are the Son of God. I believe that You were raised from the dead and are alive forevermore. Because of my sin I have been separated from God, but You died on the cross and rose to life again to make it possible for me to be forgiven. While on the cross You paid the price for my sin. You have made it possible for me to now receive forgiveness of sins. Today, I choose to receive Your forgiveness and grace. Please come into my heart and forgive me of all my sins. From this moment on I surrender my life to follow You. I confess with my mouth that You are the Lord, the Son of God, and I receive You as my Lord and Savior.

Now lift your hands and begin to praise God for saving you. From the bottom of your heart give Him thanks for saving you. Now that you belong to Jesus, allow Him to fill you to overflowing with His Holy Spirit. The following Scriptures speak of being filled with the Holy Spirit and speaking in other tongues.

> *And they were all filled with the Holy Spirit and began to speak with other tongues, as the Spirit gave them utterance* (Acts 2:4).

> *When Paul had laid his hands upon them, the Holy Spirit came on them; and they spoke with tongues and prophesied* (Acts 19:6).

Now ask the Heavenly Father to fill you with His Holy Spirit by praying the following prayer.

> *Heavenly Father, please fill me with Your precious Holy Spirit so that I may speak in tongues and worship You all the days of my life. Let me receive the fullness of Your Spirit now.*

Open your mouth and begin to speak in the new heavenly language that the Holy Spirit has given you. Let the new utterance come forth, not your own language, but the language the Holy Spirit gives you. Don't be concerned about how it sounds. It might not make sense to your mind, but it is your spirit communicating with God, and God understands everything you are speaking. Speak this out for one minute without stopping. Whenever you speak in tongues you will find that God will strengthen and refresh you.

Praise the Lord! You are now a Spirit-filled Christian on your way to heaven. Every day speak in tongues so that you will be strong in your walk with God. Now that you belong to Jesus, ask your Heavenly Father to help you find a new church home so that you can grow spiritually and continue your spiritual pilgrimage toward heaven. The Holy Spirit will lead you as you search for the Christian church that God wants you to be part of. Look for a church where you can sense the love of God and where people take a genuine interest in your spiritual growth. Seek out a church that believes the whole Bible and preaches it without compromise.

And always remember—*God loves you.*

Ministry Partner Information

We would like to share with you a sincere and open invitation to partner with the life-changing ministry of Steven Brooks International. With the support of our precious Ministry Partners, Pastor Steven and Kelly are empowered to reach further into the nations of the world with God's Word and His healing touch. Working together, we can experience a greater impact for the fulfillment of the Great Commission. With a world population having surpassed the staggering number of seven billion souls, the need has never been greater for anointed biblical teaching coupled with genuine manifestations of God's power to strengthen the church.

Pastor Steven's life is dedicated to the apostolic cause of ministering the bread of life to hungry souls around the world. Without the help of dedicated Ministry Partners, the great outreaches of this ministry would not be possible. The help of each Ministry Partner is vital. Whether the support is large or if it is the widow's last two pennies, every bit helps in this worldwide outreach. With your prayers and generous financial support, we are continuing to go through the unprecedented doors of opportunity that the Lord is opening for this ministry.

Pastor Steven and Kelly absolutely treasure their Ministry Partners. Each Ministry Partner is viewed as a special gift from God and is highly valued. Pastor Steven and Kelly believe in covenant relationships and understand the emphasis and blessing that God places upon such divine connections. In this end-time hour, God is joining those with like hearts to stand together in this sacred work. Thank you for prayerfully considering becoming a Ministry Partner. We encourage you to take the step and join this exciting and rewarding journey with us. Together we can make an eternal difference in the lives of precious souls, enabling us to have an expectancy to hear the Lord's voice on that blessed day, saying, "Well done, thou good and faithful servant."

As a Ministry Partner, your undertaking is to pray for Pastor Steven, his family, and his ministry on a regular basis and support his ministry with a monthly financial contribution.

As a Ministry Partner, you will receive the following benefits:

- Impartation that is upon Pastor Steven's life to be upon you to help you accomplish what God has called you to do.

- Consistent prayer for you by Pastor Steven.

- Monthly Ministry Partner newsletter to build your faith and feed your spirit.

- Mutual faith in God for His best return on all your giving.

- Eternal share in the heavenly rewards obtained through this ministry.

BECOME A MINISTRY PARTNER NOW!

Name _____

Address _____

Phone Number _____

Email Address _____

_____ Yes, Pastor Steven. I join with you in Ministry Partnership and I (we) stand with you as you continue to preach the gospel to all the earth and usher in the return of the Lord Jesus Christ.

Please mail your information to:

Steven Brooks International
PO Box 717
Moravian Falls, NC 28654

You may also become a Ministry Partner by registering at our online Web site at: www.stevenbrooks.org. Once there, please click on the "Partner" link to sign up.

For booking information and upcoming meetings regarding Steven Brooks International and service times at The Holy Place Worship Center, please visit our Web site at: www.stevenbrooks.org or email us at: info@stevenbrooks.org.

ABOUT THE AUTHOR

The ministry of Steven and Kelly Brooks reaches multitudes of souls around the world. Steven is widely known for his ability to teach God's Word in a clear and understandable way to new believers, as well as to those who have been in the faith for decades. He walks in a remarkable gift of *working of miracles,* and *divine healing* is a trademark of his ministry. Steven stresses the importance of faith in God and the eternal value of living a life of prayer and holiness. His heart is to see the lost saved and the church strengthened.

Brother Steven stands by grace in the ministry office of the modern-day apostle. As a *sent one,* he is constantly traveling far and wide, throughout America and to the most remote areas of the world, preaching the good news of Jesus Christ. Whether in the Himalayan Mountain region or along the Nile River in Africa, Brother Steven has a mandate from God to, *"Go, and teach all nations."* His pulpit messages are streamed live on the Internet from The Holy Place Worship Center, and are viewed weekly in over seventy nations.

He is a prolific writer; his books are available in bookstores nationwide. They have been translated into various languages and are widely distributed overseas.

Steven is senior pastor and co-founder, along with his wife, Kelly, of The Holy Place Worship Center in Moravian Falls, North Carolina. This thriving and dynamic church is considered a hub of revival and under an open heaven. Guests from other countries frequently visit and the sick travel for miles to attend in anticipation of receiving God's healing power. The church is known for its strong prayer foundations and for an atmosphere of love and humility.